Rejoice!

Rejoice!
Philippians

This inductive Bible study is designed for individual, small group, or classroom use. A leader's guide with full lesson plans and the answers to the Bible study questions is available from Regular Baptist Press. Order RBP1690 online at www.regularbaptistpress.org, e-mail orders@rbpstore.org, call toll-free at 1-800-727-4440, or contact your distributor.

REGULAR BAPTIST PRESS
1300 North Meacham Road
Schaumburg, Illinois 60173-4806

*The King James Version is the English translation used
in our Sunday School curriculum.*

The Doctrinal Basis of Our Curriculum
A more detailed statement with references is available upon request.

- The verbal, plenary inspiration of the Scriptures
- Only one true God
- The Trinity of the Godhead
- The Holy Spirit and His ministry
- The personality of Satan
- The Genesis account of creation
- Original sin and the fall of man
- The virgin birth of Christ
- Salvation through faith in the shed blood of Christ
- The bodily resurrection and priesthood of Christ
- Grace and the new birth
- Justification by faith
- Sanctification of the believer

- The security of the believer
- The church
- The ordinances of the local church: baptism by immersion and the Lord's Supper
- Biblical separation— ecclesiastical and personal
- Obedience to civil government
- The place of Israel
- The pretribulation rapture of the church
- The premillennial return of Christ
- The millennial reign of Christ
- Eternal glory in Heaven for the righteous
- Eternal torment in Hell for the wicked

REJOICE! PHILIPPIANS
Adult Bible Study Book
Vol. 55, No. 4
© 2007
Regular Baptist Press • Schaumburg, Illinois
www.regularbaptistpress.org • 1-800-727-4440
Printed in U.S.A.
All rights reserved
RBP1693 • ISBN: 978-1-59402-295-1

Contents

Preface

Even a confirmed optimist would be challenged to find positive news in a daily newspaper or TV newscast. Reports of drive-by shootings, domestic violence, scandals, sexual assaults, terrorism, military confrontations, human suffering, and tragic accidents dominate media news with alarming consistency. Heaped on top of such dismal reports are our own personal problems. The weight of all these negative circumstances is enough to make our shoulders droop, our hands drop, and our eyes drip.

However, supernatural joy is available in abundant supply. Essentially this joy is what Paul's letter to the Philippians is all about. Like a gusher, joy seems to spurt from the book of Philippians and splash right into our lives. Whenever the heat of battle threatens to dry our souls, we can refresh ourselves by drinking from the Philippians well.

Written by the apostle Paul when he was under house arrest at Rome, Philippians supplies reason after reason to be joyful. It presents Paul as a prime example of someone who rejoiced in spite of adversity. His confidence in the Lord enabled him to triumph over dreadful conditions—unjust arrest and confinement, separation from friends, shackles, and the possibility of execution. Through it all, Paul testified, "I . . . do rejoice, yea, and will rejoice" (Philippians 1:18).

As you study this course, seek to know the joy of the Lord in your life. Let Paul's words to the Philippians become dear to you—and rejoice!

Lesson 1

A Vision and a Visit

God intervenes in believers' lives.

Acts 16:6–40

"And at midnight Paul and Silas prayed, and sang praises unto God: and the prisoners heard them" (Acts 16:25).

A book supposedly published late in the nineteenth century described a world in which everything happens by chance. One day the sun rises; another day it doesn't. Some children have one head, while others have twelve. A child jumps up one day and comes down again, but the next day he jumps and doesn't come down. Thankfully our world doesn't operate that way. Our lives are not a sequence of chance happenings; God intervenes in our lives. We should recognize this fact and cooperate with Him as He seeks to accomplish His will.

Getting Started

1. When have you sensed that God was intervening in your life?

2. How did you respond?

Searching the Scriptures

God's Intervention in Paul's Life

On his second missionary journey, Paul, accompanied by Silas and Timothy, wanted to journey east and preach the gospel in Asia, but the Holy Spirit forbade this move. He also kept the group from entering Bithynia (Acts 16:6, 7).

3. Read Acts 16:6 and 7 and Ephesians 5:18. Why is obeying the command in Ephesians 5:18 so important for knowing what God wants us to do?

The men kept traveling west until they came to Troas (Acts 16:8). They didn't sit and waste time. Rather, they put themselves in a position for God to use them. Like them, we should be preparing ourselves to be used by God.

4. What steps can believers take to prepare themselves to serve God as He directs them?

At Troas Paul received a vision of a man from Macedonia. "Come over into Macedonia, and help us," the man pleaded (v. 9).

This vision was not an unplanned event. It came as a divine intervention into the lives of Paul and his missionary companions. Twice God had prevented them from going east. He was directing them west, across the sea to Macedonia. He had interrupted their travel plans and was interjecting His own plan.

The missionaries concluded that God had in fact called them to preach the gospel to the Macedonians (v. 10). Once they knew God's plan, they cooperated with God by sailing immediately to Macedonia.

5. What might be some consequences of delaying our obedience to God when He intervenes in our lives and shows us His will?

After landing at Neapolis, Paul and his companions went inland to Philippi, a leading city in Macedonia. There they began to preach the gospel (vv. 11–13).

Although it is wise to plan ahead, we must do so with a sensitivity to God's will, knowing that God may intervene and interrupt our plans at any moment. Paul's example teaches us to cooperate with God when He changes our plans, because He does so for a reason.

The Conversion of Lydia

God directed Paul and his coworkers to Philippi because a woman named Lydia lived there and needed to hear about Christ. She and other women had gathered for prayer by a river outside Philippi. When Paul met her, he shared the gospel with her. She listened receptively because the Lord had opened her heart (vv. 13, 14).

Lydia became a believer because God had intervened in her life to save her. But first He had intervened in Paul's life to direct him to Philippi and specifically to Lydia. As He did with Paul, God may intervene to lead us to serve as His instruments for directing others to Him.

6. Read Acts 16:14. Evaluate this statement: God directs us to people, not to tasks.

The Confrontation with the Slave Girl

If everything always turned out as well as the conversion of Lydia had, it would be easy for us to cooperate with God's interventions. The problem is that everything doesn't always turn out that easy for us. It didn't for Paul either.

After preaching to Lydia, Paul met a slave girl who was possessed with a spirit of divination (v. 16). Most likely she predicted the future and, like a ventriloquist, spoke with a different voice. Her occult activities directed a steady flow of cash to her masters' pockets.

The slave girl followed Paul and his coworkers and screamed, "These men are the servants of the most high God, which shew unto us the way of salvation!" This scenario repeated itself day after day. Finally, having put up long enough with the slave girl's antics and knowing that the unbelieving Gentiles might relate her statements to their own gods and their own salvation, in the name of Jesus Christ Paul commanded the spirit to come out of her. Overwhelmed by the authority of Jesus' name, the evil spirit departed from the girl (vv. 17, 18).

7. Read Acts 16:16–18. What did Satan hope to accomplish through the possessed girl?

Paul viewed the demon-possessed girl not as the enemy but as a tool of the real enemy—Satan. Paul didn't attack her but allowed God to use him to deliver her.

8. How does this incident support the teaching in Luke 6:27 and 28 and Romans 12:20 and 21?

9. How should believers respond to opposition as they seek to carry out God's will?

Although Paul's casting out the demon was for the slave girl's good, it was bad for her masters' business. Their source of income dried up, and their tempers flared. They seized Paul and Silas and dragged them into the marketplace (Acts 16:19).

The slave masters accused Paul and Silas of two things. They alleged first that the missionaries "exceedingly trouble our city" (v. 20) and second that the missionaries taught "customs, which are not lawful for us to receive, neither to observe" (v. 21). The second charge probably confused the missionaries' evangelism with the act of converting Romans to Judaism. These charges were extremely serious, because the Romans insisted on peace and order in their colonies and forbade Jewish proselytism.

The charges were a smoke screen. The slave masters weren't concerned for Roman law and order; they simply wanted revenge for the loss of their lucrative business.

The slave masters won their case in a kangaroo court. The people joined in an attack against Paul and Silas. The magistrates responded to the mob action by commanding the officers to beat Paul and Silas and cast them into prison (vv. 22, 23).

From a human perspective, no good had come from the exorcism. God had intervened in the girl's life, but two of His servants were in prison. Their feet were held fast in wooden blocks (v. 24), and the pain from the beatings was excruciating.

People of weak faith might reason that cooperating with God doesn't pay. After all, Paul and Silas's cooperation had landed the two men in a heap of trouble.

10. Have you ever attempted to do God's will and ended up in "trouble"? How did you feel? How did you respond?

The Conversion of the Jailer

Paul and Silas were men of faith. They didn't blame God for their circumstances. They prayed and praised God in song (v. 25).

11. Read Acts 16:25. What do you suppose Paul and Silas prayed about?

12. What do you suppose they sang about?

Because the word "heard" (v. 25) means "listened with interest," we know that the prisoners didn't object to the singing, even though it was a midnight concert.

13. Why would the prisoners be so attentive to what Paul and Silas were praying and singing about?

What a testimony! Paul and Silas were doing God's will and ended up in prison. Nevertheless, they were praying and praising God. Many believers today complain if their pastor's sermon goes ten minutes long. Such "suffering" is rather pathetic.

14. What might be true of those who talk more about their "suffering" for God than they do about God Himself?

God caused an amazing thing to happen in the Philippian jail. A sudden earthquake jolted the prison. The doors of the prison flew open, and the prisoners' chains broke loose from the prison walls (v. 26).

The jailer was ready to kill himself because he thought the prisoners had escaped. He knew the magistrates would kill him for losing the prisoners (v. 27).

However, before the jailer had time to commit suicide, Paul intervened. "Do thyself no harm: for we are all here!" he shouted (v. 28). Paul passed up the opportunity to escape from prison. Instead he stayed to help the Philippian jailer out of his prison—the prison of sin. In reality, the earthquake was for the jailer's benefit, not Paul and Silas's. The open doors let the jailer come down into the prison and find freedom for his soul. Trembling, he fell at the missionaries' feet and asked, "Sirs, what must I do to be saved?" (v. 30).

"Believe on the Lord Jesus Christ, and thou shall be saved, and thy house," Paul and Silas replied (v. 31).

The word "believe" implies urgency and denotes the orientation of a person's mind and heart toward Jesus Christ. It does not mean "to give mere assent to some propositions about Christ." So, by instructing the jailer to believe on the Lord Jesus Christ, Paul and Silas were admonishing him to trust Jesus Christ to save him. The jailer and his family believed on the Lord Jesus Christ (vv. 33, 34).

15. Read Acts 16:33 and 34. What did the jailer do that evidenced his salvation?

The salvation of the jailer's family had resulted from Paul and Silas's incarceration. Paul and Silas were in prison because Paul had cast a demon out of a slave girl. Paul was able to cast the spirit out of the girl because he and his coworkers were in Philippi. They were in Philippi because God had intervened in their lives and directed them to Philippi. Interesting sequence! God worked in the missionaries' lives, and they cooperated with Him.

But the story of the missionaries' visit to Philippi didn't end with the conversion of the jailer and his family members. Paul and Silas were still in prison.

The Confrontation with the Magistrates

Perhaps because of a lack of evidence against Paul and Silas, the magistrates decided to release them from prison (v. 35). They sent word to the jailer to let them go. However, their release didn't go smoothly. Paul and Silas had been condemned and beaten without a trial. To make matters worse, they were Roman citizens. Roman citizens were exempt from beatings and guaranteed a fair trial. So Paul refused to leave the prison unless the magistrates came in person and escorted them out of the prison (vv. 36, 37).

16. Why didn't Paul and Silas tell the magistrates they were Roman citizens before they were beaten?

When Paul's demands reached the magistrates, they feared—and rightly so; they had wrongly beaten Roman citizens (v. 38). Timidly they went to the prison, escorted Paul and Silas from the prison, and urged them to leave Philippi (v. 39). The missionaries complied with the request, but first they went to Lydia's home, where they met with the believers and encouraged them (v. 40).

The jailer most likely joined the group of believers who regularly met in Lydia's house. No doubt he shared again and again his powerful testimony of God's intervention in Paul's life in order to reach him.

17. How do believers' testimonies of God's intervention on their behalf affect a church?

In time, the infant church at Philippi became a thriving church of "saints in Christ Jesus . . . with the bishops and deacons" (Philippians 1:1). God's interventions are always well timed and purposeful. Things do not just happen.

Making It Personal

18. What has happened recently that may signify God's intervention in your life?

19. Examine your life before God. Do you have an attitude of co-operation or resistance as He intervenes in your life?

20. Commit to following God and cooperating with Him no matter how and where He leads you.

21. Memorize Acts 16:25 as a reminder of Paul and Silas's shining example.

Lesson 2

God's Workforce

*God expects believers to work together
for Him in love.*

Philippians 1:1–11

**"And this I pray, that your love may abound yet
more and more in knowledge and in all judgment; that ye may approve things that are excellent; that ye may be sincere and without offence
till the day of Christ" (Philippians 1:9, 10).**

Longfellow wrote, "Life is real! life is earnest!" He was right.
God didn't put us on the earth primarily to have fun, although having fun seems to be the chief ambition of many. God put us
here to honor Him, and that noble purpose involves dedicated work.

This responsibility affects our everyday lives and the life of our local churches. For the church to carry out the work of the gospel, Christians must work together. For Christians to work together, they must
love one another. It follows, then, that we need the other believers in
our churches so we can all work together in the gospel.

In his letter to the Philippians, Paul endeavored to forge a strong
link between Christian love and cooperation in their church.

Getting Started

1. What is the biggest threat to cooperation in your church?

2. What might happen to a church if its chief ambition was to have fun together?

Searching the Scriptures

Paul's Greeting to the Philippians

As he did in each of his letters, Paul began his correspondence by identifying himself as the sender and by greeting the recipients. In his letter to the Philippians, he included Timothy's name with his own as the senders (Philippians 1:1). Perhaps he included Timothy's name because he planned to send Timothy to Philippi soon.

3. Read Philippians 1:1.

a. What did Paul call himself?

b. What other title might Paul have chosen? (See Ephesians 1:1 and Colossians 1:1.)

The word Paul used for "servants" signifies slaves. Slaves were considered possessions. Their masters made their decisions, established their schedules, and told them what to do. Masters owned and controlled their slaves. Paul and Timothy were slaves of Jesus Christ. They gladly submitted to His control. They did what He told them to do. Although they figured prominently in the life and ministry of the early church, they regarded themselves as servants—slaves. How different their attitude was from that of so many today, particularly those who occupy prominent positions and expect to be served rather than to serve.

4. How might Paul's reference to himself as a slave have affected the spirit of cooperation in the Philippian church?

Paul described the Philippians as "saints" (v. 1). Contrary to popular belief, saints are not holy people who have died and gone to Heaven and later been canonized by a church. When Paul used the word "saints," he was writing to living Christians in Philippi. The word means "set apart unto God." The Philippian Christians were set apart unto God "in Christ Jesus."

If you are a Christian, you, too, are a saint. When you trusted in Christ as your Savior, the Holy Spirit set you apart in Christ.

5. What potential barriers between believers does being fellow saints break down?

Our behavior should reflect the truth that we have been set apart unto God. Our ambitions, attitudes, actions, vocabulary, and views should be different from those who have not been set apart.

Paul's Gratitude for the Philippians

After greeting the Philippians in his traditional manner—"Grace be unto you, and peace"—Paul indicated that he thanked God for them "upon every remembrance." When he thought about the Philippians, he thanked God for them and joyfully prayed for them (vv. 2–4).

6. Read Philippians 1:3. Why did Paul thank God instead of the Philippians when he thought about them?

What do we do when we think about other Christians? Do we thank God for them? Do we pray for them? If we thank God for other believers and pray for them when we think about them, our attitudes toward them keep improving. They take a positive position in our hearts and minds instead of a negative one.

Why did Paul thank God for the Philippians? He was thankful for their "fellowship in the gospel" (v. 5). Paul was not reflecting upon time spent with the Philippians over coffee and cookies. The word "fellowship" means "partnership"—a joint participation in the Lord's work. The

Philippians had fellowshipped with Paul by supporting his ministry. Specifically, the Philippians had sent him money "from the first day until now" (v. 5). They had cooperated with him from the time he visited Philippi.

7. Read Acts 16:14, 15, 33, 34, and 40. What did Lydia and the jailer do to partner with Paul on their "first days" as believers?

8. What does their participation tell you about who is able to partner in the ministry of the gospel?

Each believer in a local church is a partner with fellow Christians in the ministry of the gospel. And each is a partner with his or her church's missionaries in the ministry of the gospel. We must cooperate by thanking God and praying for our fellow church members, pastors, and missionaries every time we remember them. We must also cooperate by financially supporting our local churches in the work of the ministry at home and abroad. Partnership in the ministry of the gospel involves serving, praying, and giving.

9. Can a believer be a true partner in the ministry of the gospel if he or she gives financially to his or her church but refuses to serve in that church? Explain.

The Philippians were partners in the gospel because God had begun a good work in them and would "perform it until the day of Jesus Christ" (v. 6). This partnership was the second reason Paul thanked God for the Philippians. The good work God had begun in them was

His work of grace in saving them, in sanctifying them, and in leading them to serve Him in partnership with one another and with Paul. God would, wrote Paul, continue His work of grace in them until the Rapture, "the day of Jesus Christ." At the Rapture each believer will finally realize, or gain, complete separation from sin. God's work in us will then be completed. Until then, God will continue to work in our hearts to sanctify us (set us apart) and make us more like Christ.

10. Read Philippians 1:6. How should a believer respond to the truth in this verse?

11. How should this verse encourage those who have given up the hope of seeing a wayward friend or relative return to God?

The Philippians were right to think highly of Paul and to send him money, because he had them in his heart (v. 7).

12. Read Philippians 1:7. What does it mean to have someone in your heart?

Paul's affection for the Philippians served as an example to them. Paul hadn't even met most of the Philippians, yet he described a deep affection for them.

13. How would your church be different if every member had all the rest of the members in his or her heart?

Since the Philippians were partners with Paul in the gospel, they were partners with him even in his imprisonment (v. 7). They didn't drop Paul's missionary support when the authorities placed him under house arrest in Rome. They didn't disassociate themselves from Paul for fear of reprisal; they stood with Paul even when ominous clouds engulfed him.

14. Read Philippians 1:7. God supplied Paul with grace so he could endure his chains. For what would the Philippians need God's grace?

Paul went out of his way to make sure the Philippians knew his love was genuine. God Himself could affirm Paul's love (v. 8). In a real sense, Paul's love reflected the love Christ had for the Philippians.

15. Read 1 Corinthians 13:4–8. Record a few characteristics of true love.

God began a good work in us also when He saved us. He continues to work in us to equip us for significant partnership in the gospel. He wants us to grow in our spiritual lives; He wants to perfect us. Are we cooperating with Him as He continues to work in us?

Paul's Prayers for the Philippians

Paul prayed that the Philippians' love would "abound yet more and more" (Philippians 1:9). A popular song several years ago suggested that "what the world needs now is love, sweet love." The songwriter wasn't referring to God's love, but Paul was when he prayed for more of it in the Philippians' lives. Today, as then, what the church needs is love, God's love.

Every baby is born with a need to be loved, and no one ever outgrows that need. Love is a necessary quality for all stages and walks of life. The young need love; the middle-aged need it; and so do the old. The church at Philippi must have included believers from all stages and walks of life—and they all needed love.

It is highly likely that some of the prisoners who were with Paul in the Philippian prison received Christ as their Savior. Those who were released from prison would have been part of the Philippian church. Being ex-cons didn't make them unlovable. The believers were to love them as much as they loved Lydia or any other member of the church.

Paul wanted the Philippians' love to abound "in knowledge and in all judgment" (v. 9). "Judgment" means "insight" or "discernment." Judgment is an essential quality in effective relationships. Both knowledge and judgment refer to the capacity to discern and make right decisions. Paul wanted love to govern both the Philippians' decisions and their personal relationships. He wanted love to influence their impressions and opinions of others. Love would enable them to overlook the shortcomings of other believers and to perceive those others as cherished brothers and sisters in Christ.

16. Record an instance in which you witnessed love shown to someone who wasn't lovable.

If the Philippians let their love abound in knowledge and judgment, they would "approve things that are excellent" (v. 10). "Approve" means "to put to the test and then to accept as tested." Things that are excellent are things that really matter. Paul wanted the Philippians to base their relationships in the work of the gospel on things that really mattered. They would accomplish this goal if their love abounded toward others.

Too often we base our relationship on things that don't really matter. We like people who are like us. We like people who think a certain way, act a certain way, talk a certain way, dress a certain way. If they don't fit our mold, we tend to criticize them or even shun them. We may excuse our lack of cooperation by saying, "If he's a deacon, I don't want to be one." "If she sings in the choir, I won't join." "If she works in the nursery, count me out." As a result, the work of the gospel suffers. Love, on the other hand, leads to wholehearted cooperation.

17. Read Philippians 1:9 and 10. What are some effects of letting just our feelings determine who we love?

If the Philippians let love govern their relationships, they would be "sincere and without offence till the day of Christ" (v. 10). They would be without blame at Christ's coming. Also, righteous acts would characterize their lives. Paul reminded the Philippians that these righteous acts are made possible by Jesus Christ. He produces them in Christians for the glory and praise of God (v. 11).

Sydney Harris said, "In the arithmetic of the stomach, half a loaf may be better than none; but in the calculus of the heart, half a love is incomparably worse than none." Paul's goal for the Philippians exceeded half a love; his goal for them was abounding love. That should be our goal too.

Making It Personal

18. Evaluate your love for others. Check the following characteristics that describe your love.

_____ I pray regularly for others.

_____ I sacrifice time to care for others.

_____ I give generously to care for others.

_____ I treat all people with respect.

_____ I respond patiently to the shortcomings of others.

_____ I express gratitude to others.

_____ I rejoice in the successes of others.

_____ I take my role in my family seriously.

_____ I help meet the needs of my church's missionaries.

19. In what ways does your love for others need to improve? Ask God to strengthen you in those ways, and then take action.

20. Partner with your family or with a friend in showing love to someone else in your church this week.

21. Memorize Philippians 1:9 and 10. Let these verses stir your heart to abound in love for others.

Lesson 3

Rejoice Regardless

Believers can rejoice regardless of circumstances.

Philippians 1:12–26

"According to my earnest expectation and my hope, that in nothing I shall be ashamed, but that with all boldness, as always, so now also Christ shall be magnified in my body, whether it be by life, or by death. For to me to live is Christ, and to die is gain" (Philippians 1:20, 21).

The nineteenth-century Biblical scholar Matthew Henry was once accosted by thieves and robbed. He wrote these words in his diary: "Let me be thankful first, because I was never robbed before; second, because, although they took my purse, they did not take my life; third, because, although they took my all, it was not much; and fourth, because it was I who was robbed, not I who robbed."

Matthew Henry was able to rejoice in a difficult situation. We might say that he "rejoiced regardless." We often find ourselves in situations we would not choose to be in. Although we can't control those circumstances, we *can* control our responses to them. If we remember that God controls our circumstances according to His purposes for our lives, we will look for His purposes and rejoice in them. Remembering God's purposes brings rejoicing in present circumstances.

Getting Started

1. What is the most difficult situation you've experienced?

2. How did you respond?

Searching the Scriptures

Paul found himself imprisoned—not a good circumstance—and yet he rejoiced. How did he do it? Philippians 1:12–26 answers this question.

3. Read Philippians 1:12. What surprising news did Paul share with the Philippians?

4. How might this news have affected the Philippians?

Although Paul was not in a traditional prison when he wrote the Philippian letter, his circumstances at Rome were far from normal. Acts 28:30 reports that he was living "in his own hired house." In other words, he was living in a private dwelling at his own expense. Furthermore, he was under house arrest there, having been falsely accused of sedition (24:5). Confined to quarters, he was chained to soldiers while he awaited trial (28:16). Yet he perceived that something beneficial had resulted from that nasty situation. He perceived that the gospel was spreading because of his unjust confinement.

Paul rose above his circumstances and saw what was happening around him. Too often we are so overwhelmed by our circumstances that we cannot see how God is using them for our good and His glory. We should look at circumstances from a spiritual viewpoint.

The Results of Paul's Imprisonment

Paul identified the first result of his imprisonment as "my bonds in Christ are manifest in all the palace" (Philippians 1:13). The word "palace" most likely refers to the palace guard, so the soldiers chained to Paul were probably members of the palace guard. Those men realized certain facts: Paul's arrest and confinement had come about because he was a Christian, and he was suffering for the faith, not for a crime. It's quite possible that several of the palace guardsmen came to know Christ when they were "closely linked" to Paul (4:22).

5. If Paul had spent his time complaining about his circumstances, what might the palace guard have concluded about Paul?

6. What might the palace guard have concluded about God if Paul had complained about his circumstances?

Paul added that other people had become aware of who he was and why he was in Rome. "My bonds in Christ are manifest . . . in all other places," he wrote in Philippians 1:13. The gospel was spreading to people beyond the palace guard in spite of Paul's difficult circumstances. God was in charge of Paul's life! He's in charge of our lives too!

7. Who would the palace guard have been able to reach for Christ that Paul most likely would have never had the opportunity to reach? (See Philippians 4:22.)

8. Read Philippians 1:14. What was the second result of Paul's confinement?

Apparently as the hand of the Roman emperor Nero began to fall on believers in Rome, a number of them had become quieter about their faith and cautious about proclaiming it. But observing Paul's re-action to persecution made them confident.

9. a. What happens to your desire to share the gospel when you read or hear a missionary's testimony of the persecution he or she endured for Christ?

b. Why do you respond in such a way?

Although Paul was unable to preach the gospel beyond his rented quarters, others were spreading the word, so he rejoiced. Paul made the best of his far-less-than-perfect circumstances.

If we depend upon ideal circumstances for our happiness, we'll never be happy. We must look beyond our circumstances and see the One Who is in charge. When we understand that God controls the circumstances for our good, we can rejoice.

10. Describe a time when God opened doors of ministry to you because of difficult circumstances.

The Reaction of Paul's Brothers

As we read farther in chapter 1 of Philippians, we develop a greater appreciation of Paul's rejoicing in hard circumstances. Verse 15 informs us that not everyone was preaching Christ with pure motives.

11. Read Philippians 1:15 and 16. What impure motives for preaching Christ are mentioned in these verses?

Some in Rome saw Paul's imprisonment as an opportunity to advance themselves. "Strife" means "rivalry," and along with "envy" it suggests a bad relationship. Paul added that those people were not preaching with sincerity but, rather, "of contention" (v. 16). "Contention" denotes a mercenary attitude and a partisan spirit. It indicates self-seeking, that is, selfish ambition. The self-seeking preachers declared Christ because they believed that by doing so they would add anguish to Paul's imprisonment. Their message was correct, but their motive was wrong.

A lesser man than Paul would have resented the self-seekers' activity, but Paul rejoiced because the gospel was advancing. While men of impure motives tried to take advantage of Paul's misfortune, Paul rejoiced. Remarkable!

12. Name some wrong motives out of which Christians today might minister.

Happily, some men preached Christ with a right motive. They were preaching out "of good will" (v. 15). Their motive was love (v. 17). They preached to show their support of Paul, knowing that he faced an impending trial. What he could not do because of his confinement, they endeavored to do in his place.

Thinking about our motives is imperative. Why do we do what we do in the ministry of the gospel? Fellow Christians may see our deeds, but God sees our motives.

Paul's Response

Paul looked at the big picture. He saw that some were preaching for personal gain, while others were preaching with pure motives. He refused to let those with impure motives discourage him. He rejoiced because Christ was being preached (v. 18).

13. Read Philippians 1:18. Why is Paul's statement, I "will rejoice," significant?

Let's review. Paul was in prison, or, more accurately, imprisoned in a house at his own expense. His ministry was somewhat interrupted. But the ministry of the gospel was not curtailed; the gospel was still circulating. Because Christ was being preached, even though Paul was not doing the preaching, he was rejoicing—even though he was imprisoned and awaiting trial.

What about his imprisonment? How was he handling it? What did he think about it? How did he respond to it? Was there any possibility of release?

Paul's Deliverance

Paul believed his unfavorable circumstances would culminate in his "salvation" (v. 19). "Salvation" in this verse does not seem to refer to Paul's release from imprisonment. Rather, it seems to refer to the future, final realization of Paul's spiritual salvation. His present circumstances were part of God's working in his life. They demonstrated the genuineness of his salvation. He was not in prison because he was a criminal but because he was a Christian. Consequently, his circumstances indicated the certainty of his salvation, a salvation that had a future aspect. Someday Paul would be present with the Lord. Then he would be free from every trace of sin's power and presence.

In the meantime, Paul wanted to magnify Christ in his body "whether it be by life, or by death" (v. 20). He did not want to be ashamed in anything. He wanted to honor the Lord throughout his confinement and court trial. He testified that this prospect was "my earnest expectation and my hope."

14. Read Philippians 1:21. Restate Paul's summary of his life in your own words.

In the storms of life, it always grows darkest just before it becomes totally black. Sometimes our circumstances seem totally black—and they may be. How do we respond when they are black? Do we remember that God is controlling our circumstances? Do we realize that God is using those circumstances to perfect us? Realizing that our circumstances underscore the certainty of our salvation, do we trust Christ in our circumstances and reflect His presence? Perhaps no one exasperates us more than the person who sees the bright side of our misfortunes, but we Christians need to see the bright side. We also need to see the right side of our circumstances and rejoice in them.

Paul's Dilemma

Paul wanted to magnify Christ in his body whether he lived or died, but Paul did not know whether he wanted to live or die (v. 22). He realized that if he lived, his ministry would bear more fruit, but he still was not sure whether he wanted to live. He was "in a strait" between living and dying (v. 23). He meant he was under pressure from two sides. He felt like a traveler on a narrow road who faces a wall of rock on both sides and who is unable to turn either way.

15. Read Philippians 1:23. What was the reason Paul desired to depart from this world?

16. What was the reason Paul desired to stay (v. 24)?

Notice that Paul wasn't concerned about getting out of his difficult circumstances. His focus was on what he desired more: seeing Christ or staying alive to serve God's people.

Paul's Decision

Paul made a choice. He put others' interests ahead of his own. He was convinced that he needed to live to increase the Philippians' spiritual growth and joy (v. 25). He assured them that he would live and continue with them; he would visit them. He would do what was best for them.

Paul delayed the joys of being face-to-face with Christ in order to further the Philippians' joy.

17. Imagine you were part of the church at Philippi. What would you consider dearest about Paul's words in verses 22–26?

Each of us experiences different and difficult circumstances. How we respond to those circumstances is a matter of choice. We will choose correctly if we remember that God works in and controls our circumstances.

We are partners in the work of the gospel. The gospel is the priority; we are not. Our circumstances can further the work of the gospel. Therefore, as the work of the gospel progresses, we should rejoice in our circumstances. Like Paul, we should rejoice regardless!

Making It Personal

18. List several of God's characteristics that give you reason to rejoice regardless of your circumstances.

19. What opportunities for service do you now have as a result of difficult or trying circumstances?

20. Write a prayer asking God to help you focus on taking advantage of those opportunities. Purpose not to fret about your circumstances.

21. Memorize Philippians 1:20 and 21.

Good Citizenship

Believers should live as citizens of Heaven.

Philippians 1:27–30

"Only let your conversation be as it becometh the gospel of Christ: that whether I come and see you, or else be absent, I may hear of your affairs, that ye stand fast in one spirit, with one mind striving together for the faith of the gospel" (Philippians 1:27).

The gravestone of Alexander Graham Bell reads,

Alexander Graham Bell
Inventor-Teacher
Born
Edinburgh
March 3, 1847
Died
A Citizen of the U.S.A.
1922

For his epitaph Mr. Bell could have selected a few of his numerous honors. He was, after all, an extraordinary inventor. Just place a phone call or answer one, and you are in debt to his inventive genius. But Bell considered U.S. citizenship his most cherished accomplishment, so he chose to have that identification engraved on his gravestone.

Likely you are proud of your national citizenship. As a believer, you have dual citizenship: you are also a citizen of Heaven. How important is that citizenship to you? Is it more important than any of your accomplishments? Is citizenship in Heaven so important to you that it affects the way you live? It should be. Paul reminded the Philippian Christians that they were citizens of Heaven and should live accordingly.

Getting Started

1. How do you respond when you hear your national anthem being played?

2. What would you be willing to do to protect your country?

Searching the Scriptures

Live It!

After Paul informed the Philippians about his confinement and shared his triumphant attitude with them, he addressed a specific need of the church at Philippi: "Only let your conversation be as it becometh the gospel of Christ," he exhorted (Philippians 1:27). Although the Philippians needed exhortations about retaining sound doctrine and about getting along together, Paul gave top priority to the important matter of representing Christ well by living in a Christlike manner.

"Let your conversation be" translates one Greek word meaning "to live as a citizen." The Philippian believers must have immediately perceived the relevancy of this exhortation. Philippi was a Roman colony, so its residents possessed both the privileges and responsibilities of Roman citizens.

Because Philippi was a "little Rome," every resident was expected to live as a Roman citizen. However, Rome didn't have to coerce residents of Philippi to conform to Roman ways. Most Philippians eagerly copied the customs and styles of their counterparts in Rome. It was, after all, a cherished privilege to be Roman and have the opportunity to live as Roman citizens.

Picking up on the familiar theme of citizenship, Paul urged the Philippian believers to live as citizens of Heaven. Just as Philippi served as a model community for the spread of Roman culture, so the believers at Philippi needed to function as a model community for the spread of the gospel.

Like the residents of Philippi, believers hold citizenship in a distant place: Heaven. And just as the Philippians were expected to live like Romans, so we ought to live like citizens of Heaven.

3. What comes to your mind when you think of being a citizen of Heaven?

How should citizens of Heaven live? "As it becometh the gospel of Christ" (v. 27). "Becometh" means "in a manner worthy of or in accord with." Paul wanted the Philippians to live in a manner worthy of or in accord with the gospel.

4. Read Philippians 1:27. Why did Paul use "the gospel" as the standard for living?

We all live according to some standard, whether we realize it or not. Paul urged the Philippians to live according to the standard of the gospel. The gospel, by the way, includes more than salvation; it includes sanctification. The gospel provides an opportunity for believers to live according to how God wants them to live. Paul wanted the Philippians to live worthy of the gospel. He wanted them to live as Christ lived.

One star in the northern sky never sets, and for thousands of years it has shone the brightest and been the most reliable guide for travelers, especially sailors. It is Polaris. Better known as the North Star, it is located directly above the North Pole. You can find it readily on a clear night by following with your eye an imaginary line through the pointers of the Big Dipper. Long ago, Phoenicians, Vikings, and sailors of the North used this method to find Polaris while at sea. Since the first century, the gospel has given flawless direction for the Christian life. If a believer's life fails to reflect his or her heavenly citizenship, the fault lies with that believer, not with the gospel.

It is easy to slip into the habit of looking at life from a worldly viewpoint instead of getting our direction from the gospel, the Polaris of our faith.

5. Read Romans 12:2. How does this verse reflect Paul's teaching in Philippians 1:27?

The world's philosophy condones, and sometimes advises, self-seeking. But the gospel instructs believers to seek first the kingdom of Heaven, to honor God and put others' interests ahead of their own interests (Philippians 2:3, 4). The world's philosophy stipulates that wealth and possessions offer security and happiness. The gospel teaches that "godliness with contentment is great gain" (1 Timothy 6:6). The world's philosophy targets sinful pleasure as the ultimate thrill. The gospel declares that true and lasting joy is found only in Christ (John 15:11; 17:13). The world's philosophy calls for living it up, because this life is all there is. The gospel cautions that judgment follows death (Hebrews 9:27) and affirms that "he that doeth the will of God abideth for ever" (1 John 2:17).

Knowing the truth of the gospel, the Christian ought to live it!

Teamwork

Occasionally we wonder how a professional sports team can have so much talent but so few wins. Then we learn that many of the team's gifted athletes lack the skill of teamwork. Success demands teamwork. Paul was in Rome, and his readers were in Philippi. But whether he was absent from them or present with them, he wanted to hear that they were working as a team, standing fast (Philippians 1:27).

The words "stand fast" probably brought to the Philippians' minds the picture of soldiers refusing to desert their positions in the heat of battle. Of course, soldiers see no reason to hold their ground unless they share common values and a common goal. Why would they stand firm without a cause? Paul urged the Philippians to stand firm "in one spirit."

Paul may have been referring to standing fast in a common spirit or attitude. He may also have been referring to standing fast in the Holy Spirit. In reality, you can't have one without the other. Standing fast in one spirit is possible only if believers are standing fast in the Holy Spirit. Standing fast in the Holy Spirit implies unity of spirit.

6. Think about the broad spectrum of people in your church. What else, besides a unity of spirit through the Holy Spirit, would draw them all together for a common cause?

Standing fast demands not only unity but also a willingness to join in a struggle. Paul advised the Philippians to strive together "with one mind" for the faith of the gospel (v. 27). Striving together is synonymous with struggling together. The Philippians were engaged in a contest as they did the work of the gospel. The purpose of their struggle was the faith, that is, the gospel. The Philippians needed to move in unison in the ministry of the gospel and to not let anything distract them.

7. For the Philippians, what were potential distractions from the ministry of the gospel?

8. Which of these distractions do churches still face today?

Paul's teaching implies that an individual's response to his or her role in furthering the gospel will positively or negatively affect other believers. A team member who does less than his or her best won't inspire others to give their best. In fact, a slacking believer is prone to slow down the pace of believers.

9. Read the following scenarios and briefly describe the effects the believer in each account might have on those around him or her.

  a. A father of three young children frequently stays home from church to do household chores while his wife and kids faithfully attend services.

  b. A Sunday School teacher waits until Sunday morning to prepare her Sunday School lesson and ends up winging it.

  c. A retired man refuses to commit to regularly serving in his church so he will remain free from obligations and be able to travel as he pleases.

  d. A mother prays with and for her children on a daily basis.

Steadfastness against Opponents

Standing fast involves steadfastness. Not only did the Philippians need to be united, they needed to steadfastly resist their opponents. Standing fast, they would not be terrified by their adversaries (Philippians 1:28). As the Philippians worked together in the ministry of the gospel, they faced opposition. Friends might come and go, but adversaries would only increase. One such adversary was Rome. Nero, the emperor of Rome, led in the persecution of believers. Rome charged the Christians with being unsocial and exclusive, with proselytizing, and with immorality. The last charge was obviously trumped up. Under the direction of Nero, Rome declared Christians as enemies.

The unbelieving Jews in Philippi also opposed the Philippian believers. They rejected and resented the believers. The Jews wanted to draw them into Judaism. Paul later warned the Philippian church about such Jews (3:2).

Of course, Satan was the Philippians' primary enemy. He was doing all he could to discourage the church and cause division within it (1 Peter 5:8, 9).

As the believers endured persecution from these enemies, they would demonstrate their deep trust in God and their certainty about their future. Those persecuting them knew no such certainty. They had no such guarantees from their fickle gods. The believers' steadfastness in the face of danger would authenticate their message of hope and would also serve as an omen, or a sign, of their persecutors' doom.

10. Read Philippians 1:28. Evaluate this statement: The best way to win persecutors to Christ isn't to appease them but to stand strong against them, even to death.

11. When have you witnessed a believer's strong faith in the face of opposition?

12. What effects did the believer's faith have on his or her persecutors?

The world has many religions, but it has only one gospel. These religions oppose the gospel. As you do the work of the gospel, you will meet opposition, and you need to stand fast in attitude and purpose. You and your fellow church members need to be united as you spread the message of the gospel. You need to stand fast against opposition.

A Reminder

Some Christian leaders teach that the truly spiritual life is trouble free. However, their prosperity message is foreign to the Scriptures. The suffering Paul wrote about in verse 29 is suffering for the cause of Christ. The more active the Philippians were for Christ, the more they would suffer. Their suffering for their faith was "given" by God (v. 29). It came as a gracious gift from Him. No believer deserves to suffer for Christ, but God graciously allows His followers to do so.

13. How do most believers normally pray for those who are being persecuted around the world for their faith?

14. Read Philippians 1:29. How should this verse affect the way believers pray for those persecuted for their faith?

15. What do you suppose God thinks when we thank Him with our lips for religious freedom but then fail to take full advantage of that freedom with our lives?

Reinforcement

The Philippians' experience with suffering was similar to Paul's. They experienced "the same conflict" (v. 30). The word "conflict" emphasizes struggling. Paul struggled as he did the work of the gospel in Philippi. He experienced wrath at the hands of the same enemies who persecuted the Philippians.

16. Read Acts 16:20–24 and 35–39. Why did Paul not appeal to his Roman citizenship before he was beaten in Philippi?

17. Imagine you are part of the church at Philippi. What would knowing that Paul initially kept silent about his Roman citizenship communicate to you about the importance of heavenly citizenship?

We, too, are involved in a struggle. However, the struggle is more within us than it is without. We struggle to do what God wants us to do, to be what God wants us to be even though we face little or no persecution.

Making It Personal

18. What conclusions from your life would those around you draw about what it means to live as a citizen of Heaven?

19. What can you do this week to better demonstrate that your citizenship is in Heaven?

20. Memorize Philippians 1:27 to strengthen your awareness of your need to live as a citizen of Heaven.

A Humble Heart and a Helping Hand

Humility leads to unity and serving others.

Philippians 2:1–4

"Let nothing be done through strife or vainglory; but in lowliness of mind let each esteem other better than themselves" (Philippians 2:3).

You may have heard about the man who was so humble that his coworkers gave him a large button that read, "I am humble." However, as soon as he wore it, his coworkers made him return it. Apparently they thought he was no longer humble.

One dictionary defines "humility" as "the absence of pride or self-assertion." That definition seems accurate. The latter part of the definition—the absence of self-assertion—is especially precise. The apostle Paul probably would have liked this definition. He certainly exhorted the Philippians to avoid putting their own interests ahead of others.

Getting Started

1. How would you describe humility?

2. How would you describe pride?

Be Like-minded

Sometimes it's frustrating to try to make certain people happy. It seems that no matter what we do, they are dissatisfied or find some fault. The Philippian believers did not have to wonder what would make Paul happy. He wrote that his joy would be complete if they functioned as a like-minded group of Christians (Philippians 2:2).

"Like-minded" is a key word in this section of Philippians. It means "thinking the same thing." So knowing what "thinking" in "like-minded" means is important. A little boy once gave a definition of "thinking" that doesn't quite fit. He described thinking as something that occurs "when your mouth stays shut and your head keeps talking to itself."

There are, of course, different kinds of thinking. Some thinking never goes beyond the conceptual stage. You think about doing some work around the house, but you never do it; you just conceptualize it. On the other hand, there is a kind of thinking that results in action. You think about going somewhere, and you actually drive there. You think about doing your income tax, and because the next day is April 15, you complete the income tax forms and mail them on time. The thinking that produces action was the kind Paul wrote about.

The word "like-minded" in Philippians 2:2 expresses not merely a mental process but an act of the will. It indicates thinking that affects a person's whole being in such a way that the person makes a decision and acts. By engaging in the same action-oriented thinking, the Philippians would experience unity.

Here's How It Works

Was it really possible for the Philippians to have unity? Of course it was; but wherever people congregate, problems congregate. Someone has said that the removal of friction from interpersonal relationships is 90 percent of the solution to the problem of how to manage people. Although the Philippian church was an outstanding fellowship of believers, it wasn't perfect. The Philippians needed to remove some friction (3:2, 18, 19; 4:2).

Before exhorting his readers to be like-minded, Paul mentioned four conditions that make unity possible (2:1). Each condition begins with the word "if."

The first condition that contributes to unity is "consolation in Christ." "Consolation" means "comfort." Christ comforted all the believers in Philippi. He didn't play favorites, nor did He ignore anyone when He graciously comforted them.

3. Read 2 Corinthians 1:3 and 4, Ephesians 6:21 and 22, and 1 Thessalonians 5:11. How does Christ often communicate His comfort to His people?

4. Based on these verses, why is comfort in Christ a unifying factor for a group of believers?

The second condition that contributes to unity in a local church is "comfort of love." Christ's love for the Philippians encouraged them to love one another. Jesus had told His followers, "By this shall all men know that ye are my disciples, if ye have love one to another" (John 13:35).

5. Read Romans 5:5–8. Describe God's love as it is portrayed in this passage.

6. Why is God's love such a unifying factor for a group of believers?

The third condition that contributes to unity is the "fellowship of the Spirit." This fellowship is the Spirit-forged bond that believers share as members of the Body of Christ, the church (1 Corinthians 12:13; Galatians 3:28). Spiritual equality in the Body of Christ was a strong incentive for the Philippians to stand together as one unit in the work of the gospel.

7. Read Galatians 5:22–26. What characteristics of Spirit-filled believers are particularly helpful in preserving unity among a group of believers?

8. What does Galatians 5:26 say will happen when believers don't live according to the Spirit? (Compare to Philippians 2:3.)

The final condition that contributes to unity is affection and outward compassion ("bowels and mercy"). Most likely these words refer to the tender mercy and compassion of Christ, which the Philippians had experienced when they trusted in Him as their Savior. In addition, Paul shared a mutual affection and compassion for the Philippians. Since the church at Philippi had experienced these qualities from both Christ and Paul, sharing them with one another made sense.

Paul believed that the Philippians would strive to be like-minded if they thought soberly about these four conditions. If we reflect adequately on the grace, mercy, and love God extended to us in saving us and placing us into the Body of Christ, we, too, would make every effort to be like-minded—to work harmoniously in the local church to advance the gospel.

Like-mindedness Described

Paul described like-mindedness to his readers. He wrote first that like-mindedness includes "having the same love" (Philippians 2:2). This description refers to the Philippian Christians' love for one another and for the Lord. Like-mindedness, or thinking that leads to action, needs to be guided by love. If not, a church will be full of people who agree on problems but don't solve them in loving ways.

9. What will happen if two believers are like-minded about someone else's sin problem but they fail to be like-minded in love?

Like-mindedness also included being "of one accord," or being joint souls (v. 2). The Philippians would share a united spirit, or attitude. They would live together in harmony. Like chain links, the believers at Philippi would depend on one another.

10. What do you learn from visualizing the believers in your church as connected links in a chain?

Paul ended verse 2 by repeating the need for like-mindedness. The phrase "of one mind" literally means "think the one thing." Being like-minded, the Philippians would strive together to reach the goals God had established for them.

11. Read Philippians 2:1 and 2 again. What action should a church member take when another believer starts complaining about their church's pastor?

Some Products of Like-mindedness

Amazing things happen when Christians are like-minded and strive together to reach important goals. Nothing is done through "strife or vainglory" (v. 3). Strife indicates self-ambition, or a lust for profit and power. Vainglory is vanity, or attitudes of pride and personal prestige that have no basis. These two attitudes presented a problem in the church in Philippi; they threatened the church's unity. The mention of these attitudes also serves as a warning to believers today to consider why they are serving God. God cares about our motives for serving Him. If we are serving God because we want to appear spiritual, holy, or better than someone else, our service won't be pleasing to Him. Like-mindedness is the antidote for the pride and love of prestige that can taint our service for the Lord.

12. What problems might those who serve God out of vainglory eventually cause in a church?

Gentle Consideration

Paul challenged his readers to esteem others better than themselves (v. 3). "To esteem" means "to consider"; it denotes having an opinion about something. Not only were the Philippians supposed to consider others, but they were supposed to consider others better than themselves. "Better" in verse 3 means "standing out." The Philippians were to think of other Christians in the church as "standing out" and, therefore, as better than themselves.

This considerate attitude was possible only through "lowliness of mind" (v. 3). "Lowliness of mind" describes someone with a humble opinion of him- or herself, someone who is not arrogant or assertive. The phrase describes people who see themselves as God sees them.

13. Read Ephesians 1:3–6. How does God see believers?

The way people perceive themselves determines how they perceive others. For this reason, self-concept is important. God has given us tremendous spiritual blessings, but those blessings are completely a result of His grace. This means we have no reason to have a prideful self-concept. At the same time, God's blessings are sufficient for us to live as He wants us to live. This means we have no right to tear ourselves down and disbelieve that God can use us in His service.

14. Read Philippians 2:3. How does a person with an inflated view of him- or herself usually see others?

15. How does a person who is constantly tearing him- or herself down usually see others?

Neither an inflated nor a deflated view of self is right. An honest view of self is what God wants us to have. For us to have an honest view of ourselves, we must see ourselves as God sees us. We must recognize that He has graciously blessed us with all we need to mature spiritually and serve Him effectively.

Not only were the Philippians to consider others better than themselves, they were to take their consideration a step further.

16. Read Philippians 2:4. How far were the Philippians to take their consideration of others?

The word "look" in verse 4 means "to look attentively" or "to take note." It implies a desire to respond appropriately to what one sees. It's possible to see a need and ignore it. Paul wanted the Philippians to pay attention to people's needs and to help meet those needs. Like-mindedness would produce a single-minded concern for others that led to action.

17. Describe a time when someone looked out for your interests. What did that person's actions do to your relationship with him or her?

A Servant's Heart

Before the days of automobiles, a man observed a street vendor's horse suddenly fall dead. The loss was serious, for the horse was essential to the vendor's livelihood. While the other bystanders shook their heads sympathetically, the man removed his hat, placed a bank note in it, and said, "Friends, I am ten dollars' worth sorry for this vendor. How sorry are you?" The man looked on the need of the vendor and did something about it. That's the kind of concern Paul wanted the Philippians to have.

Someone remarked that a person all wrapped up in himself makes a small package. Although we ought to respect ourselves, no one should worship him- or herself or live to serve his or her own interests. If you worship yourself, think constantly of yourself, and live entirely for yourself, you cannot be like-minded. To be like-minded, you need to be lowly minded. You need to begin to see yourself as God sees you. When you do, you will see others as people to whom you can minister. Lift your eyes today, look around, and see burdened and lonely people. Develop a servant's heart and help somebody today.

Making It Personal

18. If a rift has occurred between you and a fellow Christian, what will you do to try to restore fellowship with that person?

19. What can you do to promote unity in your church?

20. How have you given a helping hand to someone in the past month? How will you extend a helping hand to someone this week?

21. If you could assign a grade for Christlike concern for others, what grade would you give yourself? ____

22. Memorize Philippians 2:3. Let this verse move from your mind to your heart.

The Son Who Became a Servant

Christ is the ultimate model of humble living.

Philippians 2:5–11

"Let this mind be in you, which was also in Christ Jesus: Who, being in the form of God, thought it not robbery to be equal with God: . . . And being found in fashion as a man, he humbled himself, and became obedient unto death, even the death of the cross" (Philippians 2:5, 6, 8).

A small religious college was experiencing financial difficulties. One day a wealthy man visited the campus, where the first person he met was a white-haired man in overalls. The old fellow was painting a wall.

"Where can I find the president?" the wealthy visitor asked.

The painter pointed to a nearby house and assured the visitor, "If you stop by that house at noon, I'm sure you'll find him there."

At noon the visitor knocked at the front door of the president's house. To his surprise, he was greeted by the same man he had talked to earlier, but now the old fellow was dressed like a college president. After accepting an invitation for lunch with the painter-president, the visitor asked a number of questions about the college's needs and promised to send a small donation. Two days later a check for $50,000 arrived.

Because the college president had been humble enough to tackle a painting job, he brightened not only a wall but the college's future as well.

In a far greater way, Jesus Christ, the Son of God, humbled Himself for the sake of others. Although He was God, He became a man. Because He humbled Himself and died for us, we Christians enjoy a bright future.

Paul wanted the Philippians to serve one another humbly, so he focused their attention on the example of humility Christ set. If the Philippians emulated Christ, their church would resemble a little bit of Heaven.

Getting Started

1. If you were interviewing someone for a leadership position, how important would his or her humility be to you?

2. How might you ascertain whether or not someone is humble?

Searching the Scriptures

Be Lowly Minded

3. Read Philippians 2:5. What is "this mind" that Paul told the Philippians to have? (See verses 1–4.)

4. Summarize two or three accounts from Christ's life that illustrate His living with "this mind."

Paul wanted the Philippians to be like-minded, but he knew that like-mindedness develops only when people are lowly minded. So to encourage the Philippians to be lowly minded, he introduced the example of lowly mindedness that Jesus Christ set.

Another way to express Paul's admonition in verse 5 is to say, "Think like Christ among you." Such thinking would activate the will. It would produce Christlike behavior. If the Philippians thought like Christ, they would humble themselves and serve one another, just as Jesus Christ humbled Himself for our sakes. High-mindedness divides a church and causes individuals to serve only themselves, but lowly-mindedness welds a church into a dynamic, caring group of selfless followers of Christ.

Where's Your Focus?

Paul commanded the Philippians to share an attitude of humility. After all, Christ humbly focused on the needs of others. Throughout His earthly ministry He gave Himself in service for others. And at the end of His earthly ministry, He laid down His life for others.

In the work of the gospel, attitude is far more important than aptitude. Because the Philippians were partners in the work of the gospel, their attitude toward one another was more valuable than the talents they contributed to the work. A church may bulge with talent, but only humility makes a church a home. Talented people may entertain one another, but humble people edify one another. Talent may give a church notoriety, but humility gives it unity.

5. Name a person who is both talented and humble. How does that person's humility affect the impact of his or her talent?

Hudson Taylor, a pioneering missionary to China, is remembered best for his faith. However, he was also a humble man. When someone asked him how he was chosen for missionary work in China, he replied that God chose a little man so others could see what a great God we have. If more Christians regarded themselves as little and God as great, the church would present a clearer picture of God's grace and power.

Down from His Glory

Jesus Christ provides the perfect example of humility. He provided the standard by which Christians should examine their willingness to put others' interests ahead of their own.

Paul described Jesus Christ in His preincarnate existence in Heaven as "being in the form of God" (Philippians 2:6). "Being" means "existing." "Form" indicates the essence of something. Therefore, "being in the form of God" means that Jesus Christ existed with the same nature as God because He is God.

Paul also wrote that Christ is "equal with God." Because Jesus Christ is God, He shares equal honor and glory with God.

6. Read John 1:1–12. Compare what these verses say about Christ, "the Word," with the truths in Philippians 2:6.

How did Christ respond to His eternal position as God? He "thought it not robbery to be equal with God" (Philippians 2:6). He did not think of the nature and prerogatives of Deity as things to be clutched and used for personal advantage. He freely left Heaven and came to earth to identify with humanity, to experience humiliation, and to "taste death for every man" (Hebrews 2:9).

7. Read Hebrews 2:14 and 15. How does this passage describe our Lord's condescension on our behalf?

When Jesus Christ left Heaven, He "made himself of no reputation" (Philippians 2:7). This phrase literally means "He Himself emptied." Exactly what Christ emptied Himself of is important to understand. Some people believe Christ laid aside His deity when He became a man. However, that is impossible. As God, Christ cannot lay aside His deity and still be God. Furthermore, Malachi 3:6 states that God does not change. This truth includes Christ and His deity.

Others believe Christ set aside His omnipresence, omnipotence, and omniscience. This seems like a plausible argument, since Christ had a human body that was fixed in a particular location during His earthly ministry. Yet, since His resurrection, Christ has had a glorified body that also has had a fixed location. But no one could rightfully say that Christ in His glorified body isn't omnipresent, omnipotent, and omniscient. We know from Scripture that Christ now indwells believers (Colossians 1:27) and that He promised to be with believers during this present age (Matthew 28:20).

Another group of people tries to explain Christ's emptying of Himself by stating that Christ simply didn't use His divine attributes during His earthly ministry. This view requires a person to discount all thirty-seven of Christ's miracles recorded in the Gospels. Obviously this view destroys the gospel accounts and undermines the authority of Scripture.

The last group holds the proper view that Christ didn't lose any of His divine attributes but rather He veiled His deity when He became a man. He freely laid aside the independent exercise of His divine prerogatives and lived on earth as a servant. For example, Christ used His omnipotence only under the power of the Holy Spirit and within God's will. Stories of Jesus using His divine attributes to play tricks on His friends while He was growing up might be fun to think about, but they simply cannot be true. We know from Scripture that Jesus didn't use His divine attributes until His baptism and the subsequent empowering by the Holy Spirit (Luke 3:21–23).

8. Read John 8:28 and 29. What did Christ say about His relationship with God the Father during His earthly ministry?

Christ did not cease to be God when He "took upon him the form of a servant, and was made in the likeness of men" (Philippians 2:7). Christ could never cease to be what He is eternally—perfect God.

The word "form" in Philippians 2:7 indicates that Christ possessed all the essential characteristics of a servant. Just as He was really God, He was also really a servant. He demonstrated this servitude often during His life on earth.

9. Read John 13:1–12. What did Christ do to vividly portray His servitude?

"Made in the likeness of men" (Philippians 2:7) means that Christ became a real human being. Having a real human body, He experienced pain and suffering, hunger, thirst, and weariness. He was a human being like every other person, but with one exception—He did not have a sinful nature. Hebrews 4:15 assures us that Jesus Christ "was in all points tempted like as we are, yet without sin."

10. Read Hebrews 7:26. What does this verse say about Christ's nature?

In His condescending to come to earth as a real human being, our Lord identified with humanity. The Incarnation did not interrupt or terminate His deity; He was God and remained God, but to His divine nature He added a real human nature.

11. Review Philippians 2:5–7. Based on these verses, write a concise response to the belief that Jesus wasn't God but was simply a good example of humble living.

Paul informed the Philippians in Philippians 2:8 that "being found in fashion as a man," Jesus "humbled himself, and became obedient unto death, even the death of the cross."

12. Read Philippians 2:8.

   a. Why is the fact that Jesus humbled Himself significant?

   b. Could anyone else have humbled Christ and made Him go to the cross? (See Matthew 26:39.)

The word "fashion" in Philippians 2:8 denotes something external and changeable. Since Christ was a real man, His external appearance changed, just as ours change. If you need proof of this fact, look in the mirror. You will recognize that your appearance is different now than it was ten years ago. However, Jesus' eternal deity didn't change.

Jesus humbled Himself by becoming a man and by becoming a servant, but His humbling Himself went even further. He "became obedient unto death" (v. 8). His death was repulsive, excruciatingly painful, and barbaric. He died on a cross. His obedience to the Father and His servanthood took Him to Calvary, where He voluntarily died for our sins.

The lesson is clear: Jesus considered others better than Himself. He looked on the things of others. He emptied Himself, humbled Himself, and died on the cross. Paul wanted the Philippians to be like Christ—to share with one another His spirit of humility. Just as Jesus put others first, the Philippians were to do the same. By being lowly minded, they would experience like-minded fellowship.

The Name above All Names

Christ humbled Himself; then God "highly exalted him" (v. 9). After dying for our sins, Jesus arose bodily from the grave and later ascended to Heaven. God exalted Christ not only by seating Him at His right hand (Hebrews 1:13; 8:1) but also by giving Him "a name which is above every name" (Philippians 2:9). God gave Jesus the name "Lord," which was God's own personal name. Jesus did the humbling; God did the honoring. Is there not an interesting sequence here? Humility precedes honor.

13. Read 1 Peter 5:5 and 6. What do these verses say about humiliation and honor?

14. Read Philippians 2:10 and 11. For what two reasons did God honor Christ?

The Son became a servant, but He didn't cease being sovereign. Someday everyone will recognize His sovereignty. Recognizing the Son's position and name will all be to the glory of the Father.

A Personal Challenge

You and the other members of your church are partners in the work of the gospel. As partners, you need to work together. To work together, you need to be like-minded. To be like-minded, you need to be lowly minded. To be lowly minded, you need to think as Christ thought. The work of the gospel summons you to humbly submit yourself to God's will and to serve others in Jesus' name.

Making It Personal

15. Think about your past week. If Christ had lived your life this past week instead of you, what would He have done differently? List three or four conclusions.

16. How much of what Christ would have done differently in living your life is related to His humility?

17. Think about the challenges and opportunities in the week ahead. Plan to approach them with the same humility that Christ would approach them.

18. Memorize Philippians 2:5, 6, and 8.

The Christian's Daily Workout

The believer's life should demonstrate that he or she knows Christ.

Philippians 2:12–16

"Wherefore, my beloved, as ye have always obeyed, not as in my presence only, but now much more in my absence, work out your own salvation with fear and trembling" (Philippians 2:12).

A laborer had complained all morning to his fellow workers that he didn't have a shovel. Finally, at noon, he complained to the foreman. "I've got a problem," he said. "I don't have a shovel."

"Well, what are you complaining about? You don't have to do any work if you ain't got no shovel," the foreman offered.

"I know that. But I haven't got anything to lean on—like the other guys," the worker complained.

Sometimes we believers would rather lean than work. We forget that we need to work. Being a believer is a full-time job. We must work at it. If you're a "leaner" instead of a worker, pay close attention to what Paul wrote to the Philippians about working out their salvation.

Getting Started

1. What goes through your mind when you observe a workman leaning instead of working?

2. Why might some believers be "leaners" instead of workers when it comes to growing as a believer?

Searching the Scriptures

An Obligation, Not an Option

After portraying Jesus Christ as the example of humility, Paul once again exhorted the Philippians to take appropriate action—with lowliness of mind. He wanted each of them to esteem others better than him- or herself and to consider the needs of others. He knew, of course, that humble, selfless thinking doesn't just happen; the Philippians needed to work at it. Therefore, he exhorted, "Work out your own salvation with fear and trembling" (Philippians 2:12).

"Work out" has the idea of bringing something to completion, such as working out a math problem. Notice that the concept is working out, not working for, salvation. The Philippians were saved. They needed to apply their salvation to their lives. Their salvation would be incomplete until they applied it to their relationships with one another. The command "work out" demanded continuous action. It also demanded individual action, because each believer received Paul's command. It demanded inclusive action, too, because all the believers were supposed to comply. Notice that Paul wasn't addressing only pastors in verse 12. The command is for every member of the church.

3. Read Philippians 2:12. What is wrong with believing that your spiritual growth depends largely on whether you find your pastor's messages interesting and your church's worship music inspiring?

Not only did Paul exhort the Philippians to work out their own salvation, he urged them to work it out "with fear and trembling" (v. 12). This phrase demonstrated the seriousness of their thinking about other believers. They were obliged to be both serious and sensitive in their interpersonal relationships. The command was an obligation, not an option.

4. In your estimation, how seriously do most believers take their spiritual growth?

5. What are some indicators that someone is taking his or her spiritual growth seriously?

A Vocation, Not a Vacation

Are you working, or are you on vacation? Are you applying your salvation to everyday situations? Writing a postcard, someone described his vacation this way: "Having a wonderful time. Wish I could afford it." If you're on vacation and not working out your own salvation (notice "your own," not someone else's), you can't afford it. There's too much at stake. You need to work at the responsibility of considering others better than yourself and at the task of showing genuine concern for them. Remember that consideration, concern, and cooperation in the work of the gospel require that you work and not just wish.

Sometimes believers will piously say that they wish they were holier. Their wishes are really no more than a cover for the bad choices they have made. The expression, "I know I'm not growing as a Christian, but I really wish I were," is a cop-out. If someone truly wished to be holier and growing in Christ, that person would get to work and do something about it. What the person actually wishes for is whatever he or she has, in fact, chosen instead of growing in Christ.

6. How might a believer who only wishes (rather than seeks) to grow in Christ finish this statement: "I wish I were holier, but instead I have chosen to . . ."?

Cooperation, Please!

The Philippians were able to work out their salvation because God was working in them "both to will and to do of his good pleasure" (Philippians 2:13). The Greek word "worketh" in verse 13 is different from the Greek word for "work" in verse 12. The word in verse 13 means "to work effectively."

A frustrated boss called his new secretary into his office. "Maggie," he sighed, "I don't understand it. You've worked here only three weeks, but you're already five weeks behind in your work." Like Maggie, some people "work" but don't seem to get anywhere except further behind. It's not that way with God; He works effectively.

God was working in the Philippians "both to will and to do of his good pleasure." "To will" denotes purposeful determination. God was causing the Philippians to be willing to work out their salvation. "To do" means "to accomplish something," or to cause it to happen. God was accomplishing in the Philippians' lives what He caused them to want to do. The Philippians were not alone in this task of becoming what God wanted them to be. God was working in them; they needed only to cooperate.

In southern New Jersey a clearing exists where oak and pine timber once stood. However, whoever cut down the oak and pine spared one tree about fifty feet from the road. Evidently it was spared because of its freakish appearance. A close look at the sole surviving tree reveals that it started out as two trees, about eight feet apart at the base, where each measures about ten inches in diameter. About six feet from the ground, the trees arch and unite into one trunk. From that point, they are one tree with a common trunk and top.

Like the separate trees that became one, the Philippians were joined together with God in working out their salvation. God was exhorting them and enabling them. He and the Philippians were working together to work out their salvation.

How comforting! God was so interested in the Philippians' spiritual growth that He initiated and implemented the growth process. In the same way, God is working in you so you might work out your salvation.

7. Read Philippians 2:13. How likely is God to slack off on His obligation to work in a believer?

8. When have you sensed God tugging at your heart and building in you a desire to do His will?

9. How can you deepen your awareness of God's working in your life?

Getting Along in God's Family

The Philippians were partners in the work of the gospel. They needed to work out their salvation in their everyday relationships with one another. Their relationship with Christ was supposed to affect their relationships with other believers. Therefore, Paul urged them to "do all things without murmurings and disputings" (v. 14). Every command that God expected the Philippians to carry out is included in the "all things" of verse 14.

10. Read Philippians 2:14. On a scale of 1 to 10, with 10 being the hardest, how hard is it for you to carry out the command in this verse? _____ Why?

11. Which commands from God are the hardest for you to do without complaining and disputing?

Paul was concerned about the Philippians' attitude toward one another. "Murmurings," meaning "complaining," denotes grumblings against other people. Specifically in verse 14 it refers to grumblings that cause disunity. "Disputings" means "arguments or a mental complaint." Paul wanted the Philippians to avoid these harmful behaviors.

Lights in a Crooked World

12. Read Philippians 2:15. Why were the Philippians' attitudes toward each other so important?

13. Do believers' attitudes toward each other today matter as much as they did in the church of Philippi? Explain.

14. Would you take a friend's suggestion for vitamin supplements when that friend frequently complains about all his or her ailments? Why does complaining short-circuit a believer's witness?

If the Philippians did all things without complaining and arguing, they would present a strong, united testimony to an unbelieving society. Their interpersonal relationships would build for them an appropriate reputation. They would be "blameless and harmless" (v. 15). "Blameless" indicates being free from fault and describes a person who is above accusation. It describes a person's reputation in the community. "Harmless" means "unmixed" and refers to a person's motives. Taken together, the two words "blameless" and "harmless" picture a pure and sincere Christian.

Paul also wanted the Philippians to be "without rebuke." This word means "unblemished" and describes the believer whose relationship with God is pure.

Each of these three words emphasizes an essential aspect of Christian purity. The Philippians lived in a dishonest and depraved world (as we do). Paul wanted them to maintain a pure testimony.

Our character stains stay with us for a long time. And many times those stains come from messy relationships with other believers. Unbelievers know when strife exists among believers. The word gets around, and our testimony loses its effectiveness. We are perceived as no different from unbelievers.

15. Have you ever tried to witness to someone who had observed a messy relationship between believers? If so, how effective was your witness?

Right relationships among Christians build a strong testimony for Christ in their community. In the midst of spiritual and moral darkness, they "shine as lights in the world" (v. 15). They stand out because their character and conduct are different. While they hold back a tide of godlessness, they hold forth "the word of life" (v. 16). They keep a firm grip on the gospel, which they offer freely to the unsaved. They order their lives by the high standards of the Word of life, thereby proving that they are citizens of Heaven.

Those who hold fast to the Word of life become a source of joy to their spiritual mentors (v. 16). Their mentors will rejoice, as Paul hoped to do, "in the day of Christ."

Do What You Should

Someone has calculated that the average worker could double his production overnight if he would do everything he knows he should do and stop doing what he knows he should not do. You are a partner in the work of the gospel. That responsibility demands work. Throughout your Christian life, you are supposed to pursue a vocation, not a vacation. You are supposed to serve God faithfully. You need to work out your salvation as you work for the gospel. As you do so, your productivity in the work of the gospel will increase dramatically. Just do what you know you ought to do and stop doing what you know you shouldn't do.

In addition, consider others better than yourself. Be concerned about others. Don't concentrate exclusively on yourself and your needs.

Making It Personal

16. a. How seriously do you take your spiritual growth?

    b. What can you cite as evidence for your conclusion?

17. Describe one way you will increase your effort this week in working out your salvation.

18. Write a prayer thanking God for His work in and through you.

19. Memorize Philippians 2:12.

Three Humble Servants

Selfless concern for others honors Christ.

Philippians 2:17–30

"For I have no man likeminded, who will naturally care for your state. For all seek their own, not the things which are Jesus Christ's" (Philippians 2:20, 21).

J ames McConkey, author of *The Threefold Secret of the Holy Spirit,* used to tell this story:

> Into the life of my brother came this experience. The winter was ending. The ice in our native river was breaking up. A few miles above our home was a small town at which an immense ice jam had formed in the river. Just below this was an island on which eleven people, men, women and children, were imprisoned.
>
> Everyone knew the fate that awaited them. If the ice dam, with its great wall of water behind it, should break, it would sweep those unfortunate people down-river to their deaths.
>
> When my brother learned of this situation he put fifty dollars in his pocket and hurried to the little town. When he arrived there he found the entire population lined up along the river banks waiting for the inevitable catastrophe. Standing among the crowd he offered the fifty dollars to any man who would attempt to rescue the imperiled islanders. But no one signified his willingness to make the desperate attempt. Again and again he repeated his offer, and each time it was refused.

71

Unable to induce anyone else to try the rescue operation, he
sent to the village store for a length of small but strong rope. When
it came, my brother tied this to his belt and offered to join himself to any man who would rope himself in an effort to save the
lives of the doomed people on the island. Immediately four men
stepped to his side, roping themselves to the same line of peril.
And those five men picked their way across the great ice dam at
imminent hazard of their own lives to bring back to safety those
that otherwise would have certainly died. When he offered money,
there was not a man who would take the risk. But when they
saw him willing to give himself, and were touched by the life that
counted no price too great, he drew them instantly to his side.

Paul realized the value of examples. Timothy and Epaphroditus
were partners in the gospel with Paul. All three men considered others
better than themselves and demonstrated concern for others' needs.
Paul cited his own example and then held Timothy and Epaphroditus
up to the Philippians as examples they could esteem and emulate.

Getting Started

1. Whose example has encouraged you to become active in serving
the Lord?

2. Name someone who has made you feel special by his or her
service to you.

Searching the Scriptures

Paul's Example

Paul practiced what he preached. He considered the Philippians
as better than himself, and he was deeply concerned about them. In
Philippians 2:17 he referred to himself as a being offered up. "Being

poured out as a drink offering" is a more literal rendering. Paul was most likely talking about his present imprisonment. While Paul was suffering for Christ in Rome, the Philippians were suffering for Christ in Philippi—"sacrifice and service of your faith."

3. Read Philippians 2:17. How did Paul respond to his suffering and the suffering of the Philippians?

After sharing his example in verse 17, Paul called on the Philippians to also have joy in the midst of their suffering and to rejoice with him in his suffering (v. 18). This is a significant turn in Paul's emphasis. He was turning from expressing his joy in verse 17 (also in 1:4 and 18 and 2:2 and 16) to calling the Philippians to rejoice. Notice that Paul didn't express a hope that the Philippians would feel joyful. Rather the apostle told them to be joyful that he was suffering for Christ and that they themselves were doing the same. Of course for this to happen, the Philippians needed to take their eyes off their circumstances and focus them squarely on the Lord. Hence Paul's command later in the letter: "Rejoice in the Lord alway: and again I say, Rejoice" (4:4).

4. How do you normally respond when you hear of a missionary who is undergoing persecution?

5. Is joy one of your responses? Why or why not?

No One but Timothy

Paul wanted to visit the Philippians, but he was unable to do so because he was confined in Rome under house arrest. He hoped to visit them again; but in the meantime he assured the Philippians, "I trust in the Lord Jesus to send Timotheus shortly unto you" (2:19). The word translated "I trust" means "I hope." "In the Lord Jesus" points out that

Paul subjected his plans to the Lord's sovereignty. The Lord willing, he would send Timothy to Philippi because he wanted to be encouraged by a favorable report of the Philippians' spiritual progress.

Paul chose Timothy because he was convinced that Timothy was a man of deep concern and blameless character. Paul wrote concerning Timothy, "I have no man likeminded, who will naturally care for your state" (v. 20). By "likeminded," Paul meant that Timothy shared Paul's concern for the Philippians. "Naturally care" means "to sincerely be concerned about."

6. Why is sincerity necessary for service to be truly humble?

We often think that we live in a me-first kind of world. But self-centeredness wasn't born in our lifetime; it has been around a long time. Even in the first-century church self-interest abounded.

7. Read Philippians 2:21. What characterized the believers who weren't qualified to make the trip to Philippi?

8. Compare Philippians 2:21 with 2:4. What correlation do you see?

9. Fast forward from Paul's letter to the end of Timothy's life. Do you suppose Timothy ever regretted giving up seeking his own things? Why or why not?

Sending Timothy to Philippi made good sense. Paul wanted the Philippians to show concern for one another. They could see how Timothy portrayed his concern for them, and they could follow his example.

Does your concern for others outweigh your concern for yourself? When Jesus taught His disciples about His inevitable death on the cross—

a substitutionary death for sinners—the disciples ignored His words. They chose to deny Jesus' cross and dream about His kingdom. Hoping to get a jump on the rest of the disciples who wanted prestigious positions in the Kingdom, James and John asked Jesus to give them co-regent positions. "Grant unto us that we may sit, one on thy right hand, and the other on thy left hand, in thy glory," they petitioned (Mark 10:37).

Jesus' reply knocked the props out of the disciples' political platform.

10. Read Mark 10:42–44. How did Jesus reply to His self-seeking disciples?

Then Jesus offered Himself as the supreme example of selfless concern for others. "For even the Son of man came not to be ministered unto, but to minister," He explained, "and to give his life a ransom for many" (v. 45).

If we truly follow Christ, we will reflect His character by caring more for others than for ourselves.

Timothy's Proven Worth

The Philippians knew "the proof" of Timothy (Philippians 2:22). "Proof of him" refers to his proven worth. He had stood the test in his ministry with Paul. He had served with Paul in the work of the gospel as a son with a father. Plutarch suggested that "character is simply habit long continued." Timothy had habitually served others. That was a major mark of his character. He was characterized by concern. He displayed the attitude Paul wanted the Philippians to show to one another. Timothy's humility made his like-mindedness possible.

11. If you had to send someone on a mission much like the one Paul sent Timothy on, who would you choose? Why?

Expect Company Soon

After describing Timothy's concern and character, Paul again mentioned his visit to Philippi (Philippians 2:23). He hoped to send Timothy at once. As soon as Paul knew the outcome of his legal trial, he would send Timothy. At the same time he hoped to visit the Philippians (v. 24). Paul seemed to think he would be released from Roman custody and then could visit the Philippians without delay.

12. Read Philippians 2:24. If you were part of the church at Philippi, how might you have responded to Paul's plans to visit as soon as possible?

13. How should believers today respond to God's Word in light of Christ's any-moment return?

Epaphroditus's Concern

Epaphroditus served as another example of consideration and concern for the Philippians. Paul had not sent him to the Philippians; they had sent him to Paul. Having found Paul in Rome, Epaphroditus performed a ministry of service to him. But Epaphroditus fell ill in Rome, and Paul was returning him to the Philippians.

Paul's imprisonment had reduced his ministry opportunities, so he needed someone to help him in his ministry. The Philippians had sent Epaphroditus to Paul because they were concerned about him. Paul regarded Epaphroditus as his brother, his companion, and a fellow soldier (v. 25). That's quite a recommendation. On top of that, Epaphroditus was the Philippians' messenger.

14. What do you learn about Epaphroditus from the titles Paul gave him in verse 25?

Brother

Companion in labor

Fellow soldier

Messenger

Epaphroditus showed unselfish concern for Paul's needs. His attitude was precisely the kind of attitude Paul wanted all the Philippians to show to one another.

But Paul informed the Philippians that he was sending Epaphroditus home. Why? For two reasons. First, Epaphroditus had become homesick. He "longed after" the Philippians (v. 26). He had an intense desire to go home. Second, Epaphroditus had become greatly distressed upon learning that the Philippians knew he was ill. Epaphroditus believed he had failed his friends in Philippi by becoming sick in Rome. In spite of his illness, he was obviously more concerned about how the Philippians felt. In a display of concern for Epaphroditus, Paul had decided to send him home.

Paul informed the Philippians that Epaphroditus had nearly died (v. 27). However, God was merciful to both Epaphroditus and Paul; He healed Epaphroditus, and He spared Paul the sorrow of having to see Epaphroditus die in Rome. Paul was ready, therefore, to send him back to Philippi, where the Christians would rejoice upon seeing their friend. That happy reunion would reduce Paul's sorrow (v. 28).

A Hero's Welcome

Paul urged the Philippians to receive Epaphroditus "in the Lord with all gladness" (v. 29). "Receive" implies welcoming Epaphroditus to themselves. Paul wanted them to give Epaphroditus a joyful welcome. In addition, Paul exhorted them to honor him. He reminded them that it was for the work of Christ that Epaphroditus had approached death's door (v. 30). In fact, he had been willing to die so he could minister to Paul.

Epaphroditus was a sterling example of Christlike concern. Rather than being concerned about himself and his needs, Epaphroditus considered Paul's needs and ministered to him. In turn, Paul wanted the Philippians to reciprocate by throwing out the welcome mat for Epaphroditus and by showing Christlike concern for him and his needs.

15. Read Philippians 2:30. Based on what this verse says about Epaphroditus, how do you suppose he responded to being honored by the Philippians at his return?

16. Evaluate this statement: Those who resist being honored are often those who deserve it the most.

Some Mennonites consider it wrong to charge for helping another person. Instead they say, "I will charge you nothing but the promise that you will help the next man you find in trouble." That's the way it should be in the work of the gospel—everyone considering everyone else and being concerned about everyone else.

Epaphroditus's lowly mindedness was evident in his ministry to Paul. It enabled him to be a good partner in the work of the gospel. Paul, Timothy, and Epaphroditus were humble servants of God. They considered others better than themselves. They were concerned about others and their needs. They served as shining examples for the Philippians to follow. Believers today ought to follow their example. They were humble partners in the work of the gospel.

Making It Personal

17. What selfless acts of service have you done recently? If you can't think of any, what needs to change in your life?

18. What can you sacrifice, besides money, in order to minister to someone this week?

19. Memorize Philippians 2:20 and 21.

Lesson 9

What Really Matters

*Knowing Christ is the basis and goal
of the Christian life.*

Philippians 3:1–11

**"Yea doubtless, and I count all things but loss for
the excellency of the knowledge of Christ Jesus
my Lord: for whom I have suffered the loss of
all things, and do count them but dung, that I
may win Christ" (Philippians 3:8).**

Aaron Burr—American vice president (1800–1804), famous
for his duel with Alexander Hamilton (Hamilton died),
and known for his trial and acquittal on charges of treason—once told
a friend that when he was about nineteen years old, he had to make a
decision between God and the world. So he went into the country for
a week where he could be alone to consider the matter. While there he
decided he would never again trouble himself about his soul's salvation. From that time on, he threw himself recklessly into sin, sinking
lower and lower into unrighteousness until his life was wasted away.

Similarly, when Paul was a young Pharisee, he had to make a decision: he had to decide between Judaism and Jesus. Contrary to the decision Aaron Burr made, Paul made the right decision, one that pointed his
whole life in the right direction. He decided to trust in Jesus Christ, Who
graciously revealed Himself to Paul on the road to Damascus (Acts 9).

Getting Started

1. Relate the circumstances surrounding your choosing between Christ and the world at your salvation.

2. In what sense is choosing between Christ and the world a daily battle for all believers?

Searching the Scriptures

Rejoice in the Lord

In Philippians 2 Paul stressed the need for unity and then described it as a like-mindedness that develops from lowly mindedness. In Philippians 3 Paul directed the Philippians' attention to the need to be steadfast.

Paul began by telling the Philippians to rejoice in the Lord (v. 1). "Rejoice" conveys the idea of verbalizing praise. "In the Lord" clarifies both the object and source of the Philippians' praise. Paul's command wasn't just a flippant comment but an intentional introduction to chapter 3.

3. Besides the Lord, what other objects of rejoicing might the Philippians have had?

4. Evaluate this statement: Everyone will try to find joy in someone or something.

In what or in whom a person rejoices has a lot to say about that person. In fact, the object of a person's rejoicing will impact him or her for eternity. This serious truth led to Paul's next sentence in verse 1: "To write the same things to you, to me indeed is not grievous, but for you it is safe." Paul realized that what he was about to say was repetitious, but, he said, it was necessary as a safeguard for the Philippians. The purity of the gospel message was at stake.

"Beware of dogs, beware of evil workers, beware of the concision" was Paul's repetitious message (v. 2). "Beware" means "pay attention to" or "watch out for." The terms "dogs," "evil workers," and "concision" are all disparaging. Paul used them to describe the Judaizers, who would eventually try to convince the Philippian believers to add legalism to the gospel. "Dogs" was the term Jews gave to Gentiles. In this case Paul was using it to describe Judaizers. "Evil workers" referred to the actions of the Judaizers. Their destruction of the gospel was an evil work. "Concision," meaning "mutilation," was an obvious reference to circumcision. In demanding physical circumcision, the Judaizers were committing a spiritual mutilation on their converts.

The Judaizers' message to the Philippian believers, although apparently not pressing, would be attractive and plausible. Paul wanted to warn them again of the danger of accepting the Judaizers' demands for circumcision.

5. Why is adding works to the gospel so attractive to followers of false religions?

After Paul referred to the Philippians' opponents as the mutilation, he identified believers as the true "circumcision," the true people of God (v. 3). He described believers' worship as spiritual, their joy as being in Jesus Christ, and their confidence as not being in the flesh.

6. Read Philippians 3:3. What was Paul implying about the Judaizers when he listed the descriptions of true Philippian believers?

To gain acceptance with God, the Judaizers depended on what they did and on what had been done to them, namely circumcision. They were confident in the flesh. They believed they could please God by being circumcised and by performing other acts for Him in the strength of their flesh. The Christians' confidence, by contrast, was in Jesus Christ and in what He had done at Calvary.

Numerous well-intentioned religious people today follow the same error that the Judaizers pursued. They believe religious works gain God's favor. However, the Bible emphatically teaches that salvation is God's gift, freely bestowed upon all who believe in Jesus Christ as Savior. God saves sinners by grace, not according to their works (Romans 4:5; Ephesians 2:8, 9; Titus 3:5, 6). If we depended upon our good deeds and religious observances to get us to Heaven, we would never get there! Jesus said, "I am the way, the truth, and the life: no man cometh unto the Father, but by me" (John 14:6).

Paul Reviewed His Past

To show the Philippians that confidence in the flesh made no sense, Paul listed his "fleshly" accomplishments. He was not boasting; he was simply illustrating from his own experience the fallacy of trusting in the flesh. If anyone thought he had a reason to trust in his flesh, Paul had more reasons (Philippians 3:4). Paul mentioned his pedigree and his personal achievements.

Paul's Pre-Conversion Religious Pedigree
(Philippians 3:5, 6)

Paul's Statement	Meaning of Statement
"circumcised the eighth day"	He was a Jew by birth, not a proselyte.
"of the stock of Israel"	He was born into the Chosen People.
"of the tribe of Benjamin"	He belonged to the highest aristocracy of Israel.
"an Hebrew of the Hebrews"	He was the son of Hebrew parents; he continued using the Hebrew language when many others no longer did.
"as touching the law, a Pharisee"	He belonged to the most orthodox party in Judaism.
"concerning zeal, persecuting the church"	He organized a program to oppress and hassle believers.
"touching the righteousness which is in the law, blameless"	From the perspective of the Pharisees, he was free from fault.

From Profits to Loss

All the credentials and deeds Paul had boasted about and that he had considered "gain," he counted "loss for Christ" (v. 7). "Gain" is an accounting term for profits. If Paul had been an accountant, at one time he would have put his religious pedigree and personal accomplishments in the profits column. However, when Christ confronted him on the Damascus Road, he changed his outlook and considered them loss.

7. Read Philippians 3:7. Why did Paul consider his credentials a loss? Think about all the time he invested in being a Pharisee. Think about the people he must have influenced as a Pharisee. (See Matthew 15:14.)

8. Read Acts 9:4 and 5. Sum up what Christ thought about Paul's standing as a Pharisee.

Paul expanded his earlier statement by writing that he continually counted "all things but loss" (Philippians 3:8).

9. Read Philippians 3:8. What are some of the "all things," besides his credentials listed in verses 5 and 6, that Paul counted as loss? (See 1 Corinthians 4:11–13 and Acts 16:20–24.)

Paul's motivation for counting all things loss was "the excellency of the knowledge of Christ Jesus my Lord" (Philippians 3:8). "Excellency" means "surpassing greatness" and refers to Paul's intimate communion with Jesus Christ. Paul even counted all things that got in his way of knowing Christ as "dung," meaning "refuse," or "rubbish." The bottom line of Paul's financial statement had changed. Christ had become Paul's gain.

Paul also wanted to "be found in him" (v. 9). This statement seems to point to the time of the Lord's return for the church. Paul anticipated being found in vital union with Christ at that time. In the meantime, being found in Christ also meant that Paul had the righteousness of Christ accredited to his account.

Righteousness is the state of being in a morally pure relationship with God. Righteousness isn't a result of any action on our part. Our righteousness is worthless and indelibly tainted with the rottenness of sin.

10. Read Matthew 23:25–28. Record what Christ said about the righteousness of the Pharisees.

11. What does Isaiah 64:6 say about the righteousness of us all?

Paul wanted to be found in Christ, not having his own righteousness (Philippians 3:9). Paul's own righteousness resulted from human effort. Its source was the law, and it sprung from believing that he was keeping the law. "The righteousness which is of God" comes from God as a gift. It is received by faith—"through the faith of Christ." Righteousness cannot be achieved, but it can be received by placing one's faith in Christ.

12. Evaluate this statement: Those who are hardest to win to Christ are those who believe they are righteous through their good deeds.

Purposeful Living

Paul revealed his ultimate goal. He counted all things loss for Christ so he might know Him (v. 10). Paul was saved and united with Christ, but he wanted to experience and enjoy union with Christ more fully. He wanted to know Christ more fully.

Perhaps we can compare Paul's relationships with Christ to a husband and wife's relationship from the time of their wedding and throughout their marriage. At a wedding, a man becomes united with his wife. Throughout the marriage, the couple want to experience and enjoy this union more fully. They want their marriage to be a growing relationship. This is what Paul wanted in his relationship with Christ.

13. What will happen to a believer's life if that believer doesn't make it a point to know Christ more?

Paul would come to know Christ more fully by experiencing "the power of his resurrection, and the fellowship of his sufferings" (v. 10). Paul was referring to two related experiences. The power of Christ's resurrection was the same power that operated in Paul's life, enabling him to lead a new and God-honoring life. Paul prayed that the Ephesian church might know God's resurrection power (Ephesians 1:19, 20). This new life wasn't trouble free though. As Paul tried to obey God, he suffered. He was a partner in the sufferings of Christ.

14. Read Philippians 3:10 and Ephesians 1:19 and 20. What should these verses do to a believer's confidence as he or she seeks to live for God?

When Paul wrote to the Philippians, he was suffering imprisonment because of his relationship with Christ. But he suffered willingly, knowing that his sufferings reflected the kind of self-denial that Christ showed by dying on the cross (v. 10).

We come to know people better by walking in their shoes. As we experience what they experience, we understand them better. Paul wanted to experience living like Christ, suffering like Christ, and dying like Christ so he could know Christ better.

15. What can a believer learn about Christ by suffering for Him?

Coming to know Christ better after salvation is similar to coming to know your spouse better after your wedding. And you can never be happily married until you divorce yourself. In the same way you can never come to know Christ until you die to selfish desires and ambitions.

Eternity: A Bright Prospect

Paul was counting all things loss that he "might attain unto the resurrection of the dead" (v. 11). He was referring to the results of bodily resurrection, when the process of coming to know Christ will be completed. Paul would work toward this goal for the rest of his life. "If by any means" in this verse does not indicate that Paul entertained doubts concerning the reality of the resurrection. Most likely he was simply expressing uncertainty about how he would get his glorified body. Would he die and be raised from the dead, or would he be raptured? Obviously the Lord is still tarrying, and we today face the same uncertainty about how we will enter into Glory. But we know that we will one day have glorified bodies and will know Christ fully.

It is said that Aldous Huxley (1894–1963, author of *Brave New World*) was once on his way to a meeting of the British Association for the Advancement of Science in Dublin, Ireland, but arrived late at the station. Hurriedly he jumped into a horse-drawn cart and ordered the driver, "Drive fast!"

Away went the cart, jolting over the streets. After a while Huxley asked the driver, "Do you know where you are going?"

Answering with a grin, the driver replied, "No, I don't know where I'm going, but I'm driving very fast."

We may be driving very fast, but do we know where we are going in our Christian lives? Do we know how to get there? Do we want to come to know Christ better? Paul's goal should be ours. Partners in the work of the gospel need to progressively know Christ better. As members of a local church get to know Christ well, their understanding of His will becomes clearer and their Christian bonds grow stronger. United together in the knowledge of Christ, they successfully withstand false teaching.

Knowing Christ is what really matters!

Making It Personal

16. List your major life goals.

17. How prominent in your life is the goal of knowing Christ better?

18. What one thing can you set aside this week and count as "rubbish" so you can have more time to spend getting to know Christ?

19. Memorize Philippians 3:8.

Pursuing Perfection

*Believers must progress in their
knowledge of Christ.*

Philippians 3:12–16

**"Brethren, I count not myself to have appre-
hended: but this one thing I do, forgetting those
things which are behind, and reaching forth
unto those things which are before, I press toward the mark for the prize of the high calling
of God in Christ Jesus" (Philippians 3:13, 14).**

A perfectionist takes great pains to do the right thing and to do it correctly. Are you a stickler for details? Do you act with precision? Do you want everything to be perfect? If you answered yes, you are a perfectionist, Are you a perfectionist in your Christian life as well? Paul was a perfectionist in his spiritual life, and he wanted the Philippians to have that characteristic too. We, too, need to be perfectionists. As we study Philippians 3:12–16, we will learn what Paul meant by "perfect" and how he modeled perfectionism.

Getting Started

1. What do you like to have "perfect" in your life?

2. Why is the excuse, "Nobody's perfect," not a good excuse for deficiencies in our spiritual lives? Is "everybody else" the proper standard?

Searching the Scriptures

Paul's Example

Paul wrote to the Philippians because they were partners in the work of the gospel. They needed unity among themselves and steadfastness against false teaching. Wrong thinking and wrong teaching can disrupt the work of the gospel. Paul had just finished warning the Philippian believers against false teachers who put their confidence in what they did, not in what Christ had done (Philippians 3:2, 3). Paul explained that he considered his past accomplishments as "loss" so that he might know Christ (vv. 7–9). Beginning with verse 12, he explained to the Philippians that his previous statements did not mean he was perfect; he was not perfect but was pursuing perfection.

Paul's Dissatisfaction

Paul had just revealed his life's goal—to know Christ (v. 10). Some at Philippi were probably thinking that Paul had accomplished his mission. That is, until they read verse 12.

3. Read Philippians 3:12. What did Paul reveal about himself that might have been a surprise to some people in Philippi?

4. How does a pastor's admission that he has not arrived spiritually affect the people in his church?

"Attained" means "received" (v. 12). Paul had not yet received all that God intended for him to receive, so he had more growing to do. Of course no one will know Christ as fully in this life as in eternity. In this life we will always have more to learn about Christ. And this knowledge is more than facts about Him; it involves living like Him.

5. Read 2 Corinthians 3:18. What does this verse say about the ongoing process of knowing and becoming like Christ?

The word "perfect" as Paul used it signifies a kind of functional perfection. Something is "perfect" when it accomplishes the purpose for which it was intended, or when it reaches its goal. When Paul wrote that he was not "already perfect" (v. 12), he meant that he had not reached his goal of knowing Christ. Part of the reason for not reaching his goal was that he did not yet fully reflect Christ. Also, he hadn't finished his life. His purpose of knowing Christ was a lifetime pursuit, and he had more life ahead of him.

A man once advertised that he would give forty acres of rich farmland to anyone who was perfectly satisfied with what he already owned. One person came to see him. "Are you perfectly satisfied with what you have?" asked the landowner.

"Yes," answered the hopeful guest.

"Then why do you want this land?" the old gentleman responded.

Evidently the other man was not satisfied. Paul was not satisfied either. He knew he had not reached his goal and that his pursuit of it would take him to the end of his days.

6. Read 1 John 1:8. How does this verse challenge those who believe they don't need to grow spiritually?

7. Read 1 John 3:1–3. When will every believer finally reach sinless perfection?

Paul's Determination

Paul had not reached his goal, but he wrote, "I follow after" (Philippians 3:12). "Follow after" means "pursue" or "press on." It implies strenuous and continuous effort. It denotes Paul's determination and direction.

8. Draw a simple sketch of something that illustrates relentless pursuit, such as a race car chasing down the lead car on a racetrack.

9. Explain how the pursuit in your sketch is like what your pursuit of knowing Christ should be.

Paul wanted to "apprehend that for which [he was] apprehended of Christ Jesus" (v. 12). "Apprehend" means "take hold of." When a police officer apprehends someone, he or she takes hold of that person. Paul wanted to "take hold of" knowing Christ. In other words, he wanted to achieve the goal of knowing Christ.

The words "for which" mean "because," and they introduce the reason Paul wanted to obtain his goal: because Christ had taken hold of him. When Christ stopped Paul on the Damascus Road, He took hold of him and changed his life (Acts 9:1–8). Therefore, Paul purposely pursued his goal of knowing Christ.

10. Read Philippians 3:12. Why can't any believer claim that God doesn't have much of a purpose for his or her life?

Paul's Discipline

An athlete must have discipline to win a game. A captain requires discipline to run his ship. A pianist needs discipline to practice for a concert. And believers must have discipline to live the Christian life. Paul had not already attained, but he was on his way. His life had a single focus, and he exercised discipline.

First, Paul forgot "those things which are behind" (Philippians 3:13). "Forgetting" does not imply removing from memory; it implies not letting the past have a bearing on the future. Paul viewed the Christian life as a race. He had run well, but he had not reached his goal. A runner may run well for three laps only to lose the race in the fourth lap. Past performance does not ensure victory. The most important part of the race is the part the runner hasn't yet run. Consequently, Paul forgot the part of the race he had already run; he forgot the accomplishments he had already made. He didn't look over his shoulder at what he had just completed.

11. For what reasons might a runner look over his or her shoulder?

12. How do those reasons correspond to reasons a believer might look over his or her shoulder in the Christian life?

13. When is a believer tempted the most to slow down or even stop in his or her pursuit of knowing Christ?

Second, Paul reached forth. While "forgetting" describes a runner who doesn't look over his shoulder, "reaching forth" describes him straining forward as he attempts to cross the finish line. "Those things which are before" (v. 13) refers to the remainder of the race. Paul's race had not ended, and he wanted to finish it. He continued to run. He did not look back; instead he stretched forth to break the tape at the finish line and win the prize. Paul forgot the past and focused on the future.

On the whole, living in the past is unwise. Someone has pointed out that remembering our past is, at times, helpful: remembering our failures and mistakes helps us not to repeat them; remembering past kindnesses encourages us; and remembering past comforts challenges us. Nevertheless, we should guard against letting our past influence us and slow us down today. As Paul pointed out, our encouragement and challenge should come more from the hope of the future than from the accomplishments of the past. When we live in the past, we stop living in the present, and opportunities for us to move along in pursuit of knowing Christ remain unrealized.

Paul's Direction

In addition to discipline, Paul had direction. He knew where he was going. He emphasized the need to have a goal and to pursue it. Paul continued to use the analogy of a runner and wrote that he pressed "toward the mark" (v. 14). The word "press" means "pursue." Paul had used the idea earlier ("follow after"; v. 12) to indicate his determination. In verse 14 he used it in the sense of running. He was running "toward the mark." "Mark" refers to the marker that identified the goal at the end of the race. The runner kept his eyes on it as he ran.

Like an athlete running for a prize, Paul ran toward the finish line. He sought the "prize" of completely knowing Jesus Christ (vv. 8–10). Jesus had "apprehended" Paul so he would run to "apprehend" the prize of knowing Christ. Consequently, Paul ran in a specific direction (toward the mark, or prize) without looking backward.

14. Read Philippians 3:13 and 14. How can a believer continue to "reach forward" in the following situations?

a. Sitting in church listening to a message for the umpteenth time.

b. Preparing a Bible lesson after twenty years of teaching Bible studies.

c. Meeting an old friend who has heard the gospel many times but has never responded.

d. Writing an offering check to the church after years of faithful giving.

Paul's Encouragement

Paul then encouraged the Philippians to "be thus minded" (v. 15). He addressed his words to "as many as be perfect," or a group of spiritually mature people.

15. Read Philippians 3:15. What "mind" was Paul asking the perfect, or mature, to have? (Review verses 12–14.)

When Paul issued his challenge, he used a word translated "be thus minded" in verse 15 and translated "thinking" in other places. He was referring to the kind of thinking that affects the whole being and moves the will. He knew that thinking determines pursuing. If the Philippian believers thought as he thought in this matter, they would pursue the goal and run the race as he did.

16. Read Luke 18:9–14. How does the publican reflect the mature attitude that Paul laid out in Philippians 3:12–14 and called for in verse 15?

Paul realized that the Philippians might disagree with him on some minor points. Paul wrote, "If in any thing ye be otherwise minded, God shall reveal even this unto you" (v. 15). He knew God would lead them into truth.

Paul's Exhortation

Paul then challenged the Philippians to walk according to the truth they had "already attained" (v. 16). This statement referred to the truth that Paul had expounded earlier in the chapter. Paul gently exhorted the Philippians to accept what he had written concerning perfection and the pursuit of knowing Christ. He wanted them to arrive at the truth, accept it, and apply it to their lives.

Paul encouraged them to "walk by the same rule" and "mind the same thing" (v. 16). In other words, he urged them to have a common rule of behavior. Again he stressed unity. He wanted the Philippian believers to have a unified purpose and to be unified in pursuing that purpose. They needed unity for the work of the gospel and for steadfastness against false teaching.

Making It Personal

17. How has your past affected you?

_____ I am weighed down by my past failures and am consequently making little progress spiritually.

_____ I am resting in my past accomplishments and am consequently not putting much effort into progressing spiritually.

_____ I am encouraged by my past accomplishments and warned by my past failures, but my focus is on what God wants to do in and through me now and in the future.

18. What adjustments, if any, do you need to make so you aren't letting your past rule your life and keep you from becoming more like Christ?

19. What means of knowing Christ more have you been availing yourself of?

    ____ Diligently studying God's Word

    ____ Actively serving God

    ____ Consistently spending time in prayer

    ____ Spending time with mature believers

    ____ Making yourself accountable to other believers

20. What means of knowing Christ will you develop more fully in your life this week?

21. Memorize Philippians 3:13 and 14. Consider posting these verses where you will see them first thing in the morning. Let them encourage you to reach forward every day for the rest of your life.

Follow the Leader

*Believers have the responsibilities to both
follow and live as godly examples.*

Philippians 3:17—4:1

**"Brethren, be followers together of me, and
mark them which walk so as ye have us for an
ensample" (Philippians 3:17).**

A man was driving through fog so thick that he could hardly see ten feet in front of his car. Eventually he came up behind a car that seemed to move along quite well. The man decided to follow it. Wherever it went, he went; he just followed its taillights. The drive went smoothly until the first car stopped suddenly, and the second driver smashed into it. He jumped out of his car, ran up to the first car, grabbed the driver, and demanded to know why he had stopped. Startled, the first driver replied, "Can't I stop in front of my own house?"

Like that driver, we can run into trouble both literally and figuratively when we follow the wrong person.

Getting Started

1. When has a mentor helped you learn a new task?

2. How does having a mentor or an example affect a person's learning?

Searching the Scriptures

Paul was concerned that the Philippians might follow the wrong people. Therefore, he instructed them to follow him.

Paul's Exhortation

Paul addressed the Philippians as brethren, since they belonged to the same spiritual family. He wanted them to have unity in the way they lived as believers (Philippians 3:16). He also realized that they needed someone to follow. Consequently, he urged them to be "followers together" of him (v. 17). The word translated "followers together" means "fellow imitators." He exhorted them to imitate him together. He wanted them to imitate his attitude and approach to Christian living, which he had explained in verses 8–14. Again he emphasized unity.

3. Read Philippians 3:17. Was Paul being pompous in exhorting the Philippians to follow his example? Explain.

Paul also instructed the Philippians to "mark" those who thought as Paul thought and walked as Paul walked (v. 17). "Mark" means "to keep one's eyes on someone." The believers were to notice those who walked like Paul. "Walk" refers to a person's manner of life, or the way that person conducts him- or herself. The Philippians could recognize other believers who walked in a godly manner, because they had Paul and Timothy as examples.

4. What should be true of those who are held as examples for others to follow? (See Philippians 2:3–5 and 3:8–14.)

5. Can a Christian be considered a mature believer if that Christian is unwilling to mentor or disciple another believer? Explain.

6. Can someone hope to grow into spiritual maturity without being mentored or discipled by someone else? Explain.

Why was Paul concerned about the Philippians? Why did he want them to imitate him and to note others who walked as he walked? Paul gave both a negative and a positive explanation.

Paul's Negative Reason

Paul explained the negative reason first. He did not want the Philippians to imitate certain people in Philippi, because those people walked wrongly. Most likely he was referring to people who professed to be Christians but in reality were enemies of the cross of Christ (Philippians 3:18). Something in their walk demonstrated that they were enemies of the cross.

7. Read Philippians 3:18. What did Paul demonstrate by weeping over "the enemies of the cross"?

8. What similarities do you see between Paul's response to the enemies of the cross in Philippians 3:18 and Christ's response to the enemies of His cross in Luke 23:34–37?

Paul used four pointed descriptions of those who were bad examples to follow (Philippians 3:19). First, the people Paul was describing faced eternal punishment as their outcome, or destiny. Second, they served their own desires. Third, instead of being ashamed of indulging in those desires, they gloried in them. They were proud of their sinful lifestyle. And fourth, their inward disposition and direction led toward worldly things. "Mind" is the same word for "think," which Paul used other times earlier in the letter. It denotes the kind of thinking that affects the will, that causes people to live a certain way. The term "earthly things" refers to things that have no eternal worth and, therefore, whose value passes away. The people Paul described were concerned about earthly things.

9. Read Philippians 3:19. What did Paul demonstrate in his pointed descriptions of "the enemies of the cross"?

Our thinking causes us to live a certain way or to do certain things. Our walk results from our will. Our willing comes from our thinking. Therefore, we need to guard what we think about (cf. Romans 12:2; Ephesians 4:17; 1 Peter 1:13). Later in Philippians Paul made the connection between thinking and following his example (4:8, 9).

10. Read Philippians 4:8 and 9. What word would you use to summarize the kind of thinking Paul taught and modeled?

Paul's Positive Reason

Paul continued in Philippians 3:20 to state the positive reason for wanting the Philippians to imitate him and to note others who walked as he walked. He explained that the Philippians' "conversation is in heaven." "Conversation" means "commonwealth"; it points to the location of someone's citizenship. The Philippians lived in Philippi, but they were citizens of Heaven. Paul's statement in verse 20 had great meaning for the Philippians. Although they lived in Philippi, they were citizens of Rome. Therefore, they understood Paul's reasoning about living in Philippi as citizens of Heaven. Just as their conduct matched their Roman citizenship, their conduct was to match their heavenly citizenship.

Because the Philippian believers were citizens of Heaven, they were looking for Christ to return from there (v. 20). "Look" means "await eagerly"; it expresses eager anticipation. The hope of Christ's return is a motivating force. Paul wanted the Philippian believers to look for Christ's return and to live in anticipation of His coming.

11. Read Philippians 3:20. Write the name of someone you know who is eagerly awaiting the return of the Savior. What qualities characterize that person's life?

On one of his exploration trips to the Arctic, Sir Ernest Henry Shackleton, an Irish explorer, left some of his men camped on a bay while he crossed overland to bring his ship around to them. He promised to return in a few days. However, dense fog and then an ice jam prevented him. Weeks passed before he could get back to learn how his men had fared. When the wind finally blew enough to lift the fog and move the ice so his ship could enter the bay, to his surprise and joy, Shackleton found the men packed and ready to step into a boat to be rowed to the ship.

The explorer asked the men how it happened that they were all ready to go after a wait of weeks. One of them answered, "It was this way: Captain Wild, whom you left in charge, would not give up on your coming. Every morning he would command us, 'Roll up your sleeping bags, men; the boss may come today.' So we were always ready, expecting you every day." Paul wanted the Philippians to expect Christ every day; and he wanted that expectation to affect their walk (Colossians 3:1–4; 1 John 3:1–3). Those who were worthy examples to follow lived with an expectation of Christ's return.

12. What can a person do to make Christ's return more of a motivating factor?

Paul added that when Christ returns, He will "change our vile body, that it may be fashioned like unto his glorious body" (Philippians 3:21). "Change" means "transform"; it denotes alteration into something different. The word translated "fashioned like" conveys the idea of having the same form. Christ would alter the Philippians' bodies of humiliation (their "vile" bodies) to have the same form as His resurrection body. He could accomplish this change because of the "working whereby he is able even to subdue all things unto himself." "Working" denotes effective, supernatural power. This power enables Christ to bring all things under His control. He is over all things (Philippians 2:9, 10; Colossians 1:16, 17; 1 Peter 3:22). Consequently, He is able to change believers' bodies to be like His body. Someday the Philippians' bodies, which were affected by the Fall (Romans 7:14–25), will be changed into new resurrection bodies (2 Corinthians 4:14). Paul wanted this truth (as well as the other truths he had shared) to affect their walk.

13. Read Philippians 3:21. Think about Paul's life. What instances from his life clearly showed he was living for eternity and the day when he would get his glorious body?

Once as a terrible storm raged across the Great Lakes, the fierce breakers again and again swept a tugboat that was towing a heavy barge. The tugboat began taking water, and for hours the crew seemed to have little hope for survival. All through the night the fierce waves continued to beat the boat, hazarding the lives of the crew, but they managed to keep afloat. In the morning a passing ship rescued the captain and his crew. Afterward the captain told about that long night of jeopardy and explained that one thing strengthened the crew to carry on and kept hope alive in their hearts: through the gloom they could occasionally see the lights of home.

Heaven was the Philippians' home. Paul wanted that truth to strengthen them, to keep hope alive in their hearts in spite of the sometimes difficult earthly life, and to challenge them to walk as Paul walked.

Paul's Encouragement

After sharing these truths with the Philippians, Paul encouraged the Philippians.

14. Read Philippians 4:1. What did Paul call the Philippians in this verse?

15. Imagine you are a Philippian believer and reading Paul's letter for the first time. How would you react to his tenderness toward you as expressed in verse 1?

16. How would Paul's expression of care and concern cause the Philippians to want to follow his desire for them to "stand fast in the Lord" (v. 1)?

"Stand fast" means "stand firm." Paul began by exhorting the Philippians to stand fast (1:27), and he concluded with the same exhortation. The Philippians were partners in the work of the gospel. As partners, they needed unity among themselves and against false teachers. They needed to stand firm against Christ's enemies.

Paul encouraged them to stand firm because of their relationship to Jesus Christ, which should have caused them to want to know Christ more fully and to pursue knowing Him. If they were united in this pursuit, they would walk as Paul walked, and they would stand firm against false teaching.

Making It Personal

17. Paul did not want the Philippians to imitate the wrong people. He did not want them walking the wrong way. Whom do you imitate? Whom should you imitate?

18. Through what avenues (for example, television or magazines) are you consistently exposed to the lives of "enemies of the cross"?

19. What can you do to eliminate any unnecessary exposure to "enemies of the cross"?

20. Who is looking to you as an example for living?

21. What can you do this week to allow God to make you a stronger example for living?

22. Memorize Philippians 3:17. Take following godly examples and being a godly example seriously.

Lesson 12

Together We Stand

*Believers can experience peace with
each other and within.*

Philippians 4:2–9

**"Be careful for nothing; but in every thing by
prayer and supplication with thanksgiving let
your requests be made known unto God. And
the peace of God, which passeth all understanding, shall keep your hearts and minds through
Christ Jesus" (Philippians 4:6, 7).**

A father took his two young sons to McDonald's for lunch.
As soon as they got their food, an argument began between the boys over who would get to play with the better Happy Meal
toy first. The father got the boys' attention, quoted Philippians 2:3 and 4,
and explained the need for each of them to consider his brother better
than himself. The dad then asked the boys which of them was willing
to indicate his obedience to the verses by saying, "I'll let my brother
play with the toy first." Without hesitation, the two boys pointed to
each other and simultaneously said, "You say it."

Like these two little boys, believers often think that getting along
with each other means everyone else conforms to their thinking. The
Philippians were dealing with two such believers. Euodias and Syntyche, ladies in the Philippian church, were at odds and were apparently each waiting for the other to give in. Paul gave the women and
the church some simple instructions to help resolve the conflict.

Getting Started

1. How much of an impact does personal conflict have on your life?

2. How much of an impact does personal conflict have on your church?

Searching the Scriptures

Be of the Same Mind

Paul addressed two women in the Philippian church, Euodias and Syntyche, who had been at odds (Philippians 4:2). The fact that Paul named them in the letter indicates the seriousness of their situation.

3. Imagine you are Euodias or Syntyche. How would you have felt when your name was read as part of Paul's letter?

The word "beseech," which means "beg," and Paul's repeated use of it also point out the seriousness of the problem. Paul begged the women to "be of the same mind in the Lord," which means "think the same thing."

4. Read Philippians 2:3–8. How would having the mind of Christ help two people resolve their conflict?

In verse 3 Paul addressed someone whom he called "true yoke-fellow," or fellow worker, and asked him to help the two women. The word "help" implies that the women had at least recognized the need to reconcile and that this person should assist them in completing the reconciliation.

5. Read Philippians 4:3. For what were Euodias and Syntyche known?

Paul cared about Euodias and Syntyche, not just because they were part of the church, but because they had "laboured with [him] in the gospel." "Laboured" means that they struggled along with Paul. Their reconciliation was urgent if they were to continue to help spread the gospel.

6. Are you surprised that two people who had worked hard to spread the gospel were having problems with each other? Whose fingerprints do you think were all over this problem? (See 1 Peter 5:8.)

A doctrinal disagreement doesn't seem to be the problem that separated the two women. They were both active in spreading the gospel, and Paul didn't have a problem with their taking part in evangelism. Furthermore, both women were genuine believers, for their names were written "in the book of life" (v. 3). Most likely their problem was a difference in personal preferences.

7. What would you say splits more churches today: doctrinal disagreements or personal preferences?

8. What are some ways, good and bad, to deal with conflicts arising from differences in personal preferences?

Pride was the true barrier that kept Euodias and Syntyche from being reconciled. Any solution that didn't address the pride within one or both of these women would serve only to cover the problem. This is true in dealing with conflict between believers today too. Even two believers who "agree to disagree" each need to make sure pride isn't somehow woven into their hearts. First Peter 5:5 calls on believers to "be subject one to another, and be clothed with humility: for God resisteth the proud, and giveth grace to the humble." This verse makes it clear that unless the pride is dealt with, the church won't have unity. Notice that this verse comes only a few sentences before the warning to believers about Satan's desire to destroy them (v. 8).

Throughout his letter to the Philippians, Paul had encouraged them to recognize the importance of others and their needs. In 4:2 and 3 Paul practiced what he had urged them to do. He showed concern for Euodias and Syntyche, and he urged the fellow worker to be concerned too.

Rejoice in the Lord

In verse 4 Paul seemed to turn his thoughts in a completely different direction when he told the Philippians to rejoice in the Lord always. Yet this command is indeed tied to his instructions concerning Euodias and Syntyche. Those two women were robbed of their joy because of their conflict. The church, too, experienced some absence of joy because of the problem. They all needed to have their joy restored.

9. Read Philippians 4:4. What does conflict in your life do to your joy?

To truly rejoice, the women needed to have the mind of Christ. Paul was subtly saying, "Get over the conflict and get back to rejoicing by thinking like Christ." Rejoicing was so essential for the entire church that he repeated the injunction: "Rejoice in the Lord alway: and again I say, Rejoice."

10. What word would you use to describe the atmosphere of a church that is experiencing conflict?

Show Gentleness

Paul told the Philippians to let their "moderation be known" (v. 5). "Moderation" indicates gentleness, graciousness, and forbearance. It describes the attitude of charity concerning someone else's faults and merciful judgment concerning another's failings. It means "sweet reasonableness." The word pictures a person who does not retaliate. Euodias and Syntyche needed gentleness, as did those who would be dealing with them.

Paul wasn't telling the Philippians to gloss over sin and bury conflict. Rather, he was telling them the attitude they should have in dealing with each other when conflicts arose. This instruction was important, for the world was watching the Philippians. How the Philippians acted toward one another would deeply impact their opportunities to reach the world around them.

11. Read Philippians 4:5. What does a watching world learn about Christ when believers let their gentleness be known?

Paul reminded the believers, "The Lord is at hand" (v. 5). In other words, the Lord would return soon. This provided a double incentive to let their gentleness be known. First, when the Lord returns, they will be judged for how they treated one another and represented the Lord in the world. Second, the lost world was in desperate need of the Savior. Showing their gentleness would support their evangelistic efforts and help deliver the lost from future condemnation.

Don't Worry, Pray

Paul did not want the Philippians to worry whether they were facing opposition from outside the church or conflict within the church. So in Philippians 4:6 he commanded them to be careful, or anxious, for nothing. Paul defined the boundaries of what they could worry about—nothing! The word eliminates any exceptions.

12. Read Philippians 4:6. What were the Philippians supposed to do instead of worrying?

Paul used three words to characterize prayer. The word "prayer" signifies petition; "supplication," the sense of need; and "requests," the need to be specific (v. 6). In other words, Paul wasn't advocating a generic "God bless us one and all" type of prayer. God wants us to tell Him specifically what is on our hearts. Paul added that we should make our specific requests known with thanksgiving.

13. Why is praying with thanksgiving about our problems and conflicts important?

14. Read Philippians 4:7. How did Paul describe the peace that God gives to those who take their worries to Him?

15. Describe a time when you experienced an indescribable peace as a result of praying about a difficult circumstance.

If we worry, who knows what will happen to us. If we pray, God's peace will "keep [our] hearts and minds through Christ Jesus," just as Paul assured the Philippians (v. 7). "Keep" is a military word that means "to protect by a guard." When we pray, we are in essence asking God's army to take up positions around our hearts and to protect us from fretting and worrying.

We can accomplish nothing by worrying over things we cannot control, including personal conflicts (Matthew 6:25–34). Euodias and Syntyche didn't move one step closer to resolving their differences by worrying. God was their only hope for restoring their peace and guiding them toward resolution. He is our only hope, too, when our problems seem to tower above us.

Control Your Thoughts

In Philippians 4:8 Paul addressed the believer's thought-life. His instructions illuminate his earlier command to have the mind of Christ (2:5). We could look at verse 8 of chapter 4 as a peek into Christ's mind. Christ never wavered in conforming His thinking to the standards set forth in this verse. His thinking included things that were . . .

- "true," not a lie or deceitful.
- "honest," or honorable.
- "just," or right according to God's standard.
- "pure," or untainted by evil.
- "lovely," or loveable.
- "of good report," or admirable.

Conflict between believers many times begins in their thoughts. Stewing about what someone else did or said will often heighten the conflict instead of bringing it to a resolution. Our minds will naturally create their own reality—one that best supports our side of the conflict.

16. Which of the thought-life guidelines in Philippians 4:8 would be particularly beneficial in helping a believer to solve conflicts in a godly way?

Included in Paul's instructions is the dispelling of the idea that a believer's private world isn't of consequence as long as his or her public world seems in order. For example, acting pleasantly toward someone we want to reach out and smack doesn't please the Lord. God doesn't want us to just act like believers; He also wants us to think like believers.

17. What are some influences that feed a believer's mind with thoughts and ideas that violate Philippians 4:8?

18. Read John 17:17. What will help a believer to develop a Philippians 4:8 kind of mind?

Paul did not ask the Philippians to do something he did not practice. They not only "learned, and received, and heard" this instruction from Paul; they saw him carry it out. And Paul wanted them to do as he had instructed and modeled (Philippians 4:9). "Do" means to "practice."

Following Paul's instructions about their thought-lives would help the Philippians get along with each other and bring peace among them. It will do the same for us today.

Making It Personal

19. Are you at odds with another believer? If so, what steps will you take to restore your relationship?

20. List specific concerns you have been worrying about instead of praying about (especially personal conflicts with other believers). Pray about them, and record how God's peace replaced your worry.

21. What are the outside influences on your thoughts?

22. How have they helped or hindered you in conforming your thoughts to Philippians 4:8?

Increase your exposure this week to those influences that help you think in a godly way. As you do, you will see your ability to get along with others and your ability to resolve conflicts strengthened.

23. Memorize Philippians 4:6 and 7.

Paul's Thank-you Note

*God enables all believers
to be contented, faithful givers.*

Philippians 4:10–23

"But my God shall supply all your need according to his riches in glory by Christ Jesus" (Philippians 4:19).

As a family drove home from church one Sunday morning, they had nothing but criticism for the service.

"That preacher's sermons get more boring all the time," grumbled the teenage daughter.

"But his sermon wasn't nearly as bad as the choir's singing," the father crabbed.

The mother, not to be outdone, remarked, "Two things bothered me most—the soloist's cracked voice and the way the organist tromped on the organ. I thought I'd go crazy before they finished."

The eleven-year-old son listened. Then, remembering his father's offering, he piped up, "Well, I didn't think it was such a bad show for a couple of dollars. We woulda spent more if we'd gone someplace else!"

This story illustrates the attitude some Christians have about giving. They feel as if they're paying for a show or paying admission to get into church. And usually they spend less on church than they spend on entertainment. But giving involves something different. The Philippians had given gifts to Paul, and he used the opportunity to thank them and to teach about giving and contentment.

Getting Started

1. Pretend you just won a million dollars. What is the first thought that crosses your mind?

2. What do your initial thoughts tell you about yourself?

Searching the Scriptures

Paul Acknowledges Their Gift

In Philippians 4:10 Paul told the Philippian believers that he rejoiced in the Lord because they had sent him a financial gift. In fact, he didn't only rejoice; he rejoiced "greatly," or with great emotion. However, Paul did not exult over the size of their contribution; instead he reveled in the Lord. For, ultimately, God was responsible for meeting Paul's need. God was the One Who had worked in the Philippians' hearts to cause them to give to Paul's ministry.

In discussing this subject, Paul again used a word that refers to thinking that motivates the will. It is translated "care" in verse 10, and it describes a thoughtful concern. Paul described the Philippians' care as "flourish[ing] again." It thrived because the Philippians had an opportunity to give, and they gave out of concern, not out of compulsion.

3. Is giving away money something that comes easy for most people? What did the Philippians show about their spirituality by their flourishing care for Paul? (See Philippians 2:4 and 5.)

Although Paul was thankful for the Philippians' gift, he wanted them to know that he was content in his circumstances. In 4:11 he wrote, "Not that I speak in respect of want." Then he explained that he had "learned . . . to be content." It had taken time, but he had learned it. Paul's contentment was independent of external circumstances; he depended on God alone. For that reason the Philippians' concern meant more to him than their contribution did.

4. Read Philippians 4:12. In what contrasting circumstances did Paul learn contentment?

5. What would you say to the person who believes that those who are "full" and "abound" don't struggle with being content?

When Paul learned to be content, he learned "how to be abased, and . . . how to abound" (v. 12). He knew how to exist with less than enough, and he knew how to exist with more than enough. Some people are discontent either way. Contentment has nothing to do with what you have. A person who is discontent when poor will also be discontent when rich.

Entering his breakfast room one morning, an English lord heard his cook exclaim, "Oh, if I only had five pounds, wouldn't I be content!" Eager to see the woman satisfied, the lord entered the room and handed her five pounds. She profusely thanked the lord, who then left. But he paused outside the door to hear if the cook would express her satisfaction and thank God. As soon as she could not see the lord, she cried out, "Why didn't I say ten?" She was discontent without the five pounds and discontent with the five pounds. We may be like that cook. Paul, on the other hand, had learned by experience to be content with and without.

Contentment sounds nice. But can anyone really be content? Can you be content? If Paul could be content, so can we.

6. Read Philippians 4:13. What was the secret of Paul's contentment?

In verse 13 the word "do" signifies power to cope in all circumstances. "All things" refers to the circumstances Paul had just mentioned—fullness, hunger, abundance, and need. "All things" does not mean "everything." It is limited by its context. Paul could not do everything he wanted through Christ, nor can we. But he could be abased, and he could abound through Christ.

Although Paul was content in his circumstances, he commended the Philippians for their gift to him. They had done well by sending him money (v. 14). In return, Paul did not merely acknowledge their gift; he appreciated it. Their gift made them his partners in his imprisonment and suffering. When they gave to Paul, they actually gave to the work of the gospel.

7. Do you think the Philippians were content with what God had given them? Why or why not?

8. What kind of giving habits would you expect of those who have learned contentment?

Paul Appreciates Their Goodness

Only the Philippian church helped Paul financially when he departed from Macedonia. When he ministered in Thessalonica, they sent him money more than once (vv. 15, 16).

9. Read Philippians 4:17. What did Paul desire more than the gifts he received from the Philippians?

Paul wanted the Philippians' accounts to accrue interest. He used the word "fruit" to indicate that interest (v. 17). He meant that he did not want their gift as a deposit in his material account, but rather as interest on their spiritual account.

10. What are some of the fruits of giving?

Because the Philippians' gift had come from their concern for Paul, it had "a sweet smell" and was a sacrifice acceptable to God (v. 18). Their gift to Paul for the work of the ministry was, in reality, a gift to God, a gift that pleased Him.

In Old Testament times, those who revered God offered various kinds of sacrifices to atone for their sins. (The book of Leviticus describes many of them.) God accepted their willing sacrifices; in fact, the smell was sweet to Him (Genesis 8:21; Exodus 29:18, 25, 41; Leviticus 1:9, 13, 17; 2:2, 9). However, the Israelites were never to use sacrifices as a means to buy off God with the hope that He would overlook their ongoing sins.

11. Read Isaiah 1:11–15. What did God think of Israel's sacrifices that were given from disobedient hearts?

12. Read Isaiah 1:16 and 17. What did God want the Israelites to do before He would accept their sacrifices?

13. Read Philippians 4:18. What might make a person's giving unacceptable to God today?

Before World War II a band of communist-inspired hoodlums invaded the grounds of the Soochun Leper Colony in Korea and set fire

to the church where the lepers worshiped. The colonists desperately attempted to save the building, but the fire almost destroyed it. The poor
lepers were nearly heartbroken over the loss of their church and were
discouraged when they learned that rebuilding it would cost $1,250.
However, on the next Sunday, after praying diligently, that band of
believers pledged themselves to raise the full amount by going without
dinner every Sunday for two full years. Surely their sacrifice must have
smelled sweet to the Lord. The Philippians' gift to Paul also smelled
sweet to Him.

Any time we're tempted to give grudgingly and then grumble about
the amount we've given, we need to remember Paul's words to the
Philippians. We should give out of concern for the work and workers of
the gospel, and we should give as an offering to the Lord.

14. Read Philippians 4:19. What promise did Paul give to the Philippians?

15. Can all believers claim Philippians 4:19 as their own? What must
be true of a believer before he or she can claim the promise of God's
provision? (See Philippians 4:15–18.)

16. Evaluate this statement: Those who are needy can't afford not to
give to the Lord.

Giving to God won't make you rich. Don't expect a check in the
mail every time you drop one into an offering plate. But do expect God
to supply your needs as you faithfully give out of true devotion to Him.
Also expect God to bless your life spiritually as you give Him free ac-
cess to your bank accounts.

17. Describe a time when you faithfully gave to God and He supplied your needs.

Paul's Greetings

Paul concluded his letter to the Philippians by exchanging greetings and giving a benediction. Evidently a number of "Caesar's household," or civil servants of the Roman government, had come to know Christ as their Savior while Paul was imprisoned in Rome. Paul included them, telling the Philippians that the saints there saluted and greeted the believers in Philippi (vv. 21, 22).

The Philippians were partners with Paul and with one another in the work of the gospel. They were not special people; they were ordinary Christians. They needed to mature as partners. They needed unity among themselves and steadfastness against false teachers. They needed to be like-minded and lowly minded. These changes were possible only if they thought like Christ thought. To think like Christ, they needed to come to know Him more fully. Then they would be effective partners in the work of the gospel.

Today we are partners in the work of the gospel, and we need what the Philippians needed. Paul prayed that Christ's grace would be with them (v. 23). His grace would enable them to be united and steadfast, just as it will enable us. Will you let God perfect you so you can be an effective partner in the work of the gospel?

Making It Personal

18. If you give to the Lord's work, why do you give? Check the following statements that reflect your reasons, or write your own.

_____ Because I am obligated to give.

_____ Because it makes me feel better about the spiritual deficiencies in my life.

____ Because I love the Lord.

____ Because I want to see God's work grow.

____ Because I believe it excuses me from having to give my
time to the Lord.

____ Because I . . .

____ Because I . . .

19. What adjustments, if any, do you need to make to your reasons
for giving to the Lord's work?

20. Are you learning to be content? Consider implementing the following ideas to learn contentment, or come up with your own ideas.
Check the ones you want to implement.

☐ Pray for contentment. You have not because you ask not, and
God has promised His enabling (Philippians 4:13).

☐ Praise God every day for both the blessings and challenges
He brings your way.

☐ Avoid unnecessarily walking through stores and malls, and
avoid aimlessly browsing catalogs filled with your favorite
"toys."

☐ Pray earnestly for those with needs—especially for those with
needs greater than your own.

☐ Purpose to treat your money as God's money. Determine to
take all major financial decisions to God in prayer.

☐ Evaluate your giving, and set goals to increase it.

☐ Ask God to give you specific opportunities to give above and beyond your regular giving.

☐

☐

21. Memorize Philippians 4:19 as an additional means of learning contentment.